7/03

10/
1

/03

VGM Opportunities Series

OPPORTUNITIES IN
LIBRARY AND
INFORMATION
SCIENCE CAREERS

Kathleen de la Peña McCook
Margaret Myers

Revised by
Blythe Camenson

VGM Career Books

Chicago   New York   San Francisco   Lisbon   London   Madrid   Mexico City
Milan   New Delhi   San Juan   Seoul   Singapore   Sydney   Toronto

Library of Congress Cataloging-in-Publication Data

McCook, Kathleen de la Peña.
　　Opportunities in library and information science careers / Kathleen de la Peña McCook; Margaret Myers; revised by Blythe Camenson.
　　　　p.　　cm. — (VGM opportunities series)
　　Includes bibliographical references.
　　ISBN 0-658-01641-5 (acid-free paper) — ISBN 0-658-01642-3 (pbk. : acid-free paper)
　　　　1. Library science—Vocational guidance—United States.　　2. Information science—Vocational guidance—United States.　　I. Myers, Margaret, 1933-　　II. Camenson, Blythe.　　III. Title.
IV. Series.

Z682.2.U5　H453　　2001
020'.23'73—dc21

2001026054

VGM Career Books

A Division of The *McGraw·Hill* Companies

ISBN 0-658-01641-5 (hardcover)
　　　0-658-01642-3 (paperback)

This book was set in Times by Publication Services, Inc.
Printed and bound by Lake Book Manufacturing

Cover photograph copyright © Eyewire

This book is printed on acid-free paper.

CONTENTS

ABOUT THE AUTHORS

Kathleen de la Peña McCook has chaired the American Library Association's Advisory Committee to the Office for Library Personnel Resources and the Advisory Committee on Literacy and Outreach Services. She is the author of several national studies on issues relating to recruitment and organization entry and a frequent speaker on career development. She is Director and Professor at the School of Library and Information Science at the University of South Florida, Tampa. McCook has served on the faculties of the University of Illinois in Urbana-Champaign and Louisiana State University, where she was dean of the School of Library and Information Science from 1983 to 1990 and dean of the graduate school from 1990 to 1992. Her bachelor's degree is from the University of Illinois at Chicago, and she holds master's degrees from Marquette University and the University of Chicago and a Ph.D. from the University of Wisconsin in Madison.

As an activist in professional organizations, McCook has encountered many of the activities discussed in this book. She has contributed to and edited professional journals, conducted continuing education programs, and has chaired diversity recruitment initiatives for the American Library Association's Office for Library Personnel Resources.

Margaret Myers joined the Peace Corps to work in libraries in rural Botswana in 1995. Prior to the Peace Corps, Myers was director of the American Library Association Office for Library Personnel Resources for nearly twenty years. In this capacity she was involved with helping prospective librarians learn about careers in librarianship, educational programs, and scholarships. She was responsible for developing conference programs and workshops and publications on a variety of personnel-related topics to assist library employers and staff with such issues as collective bargaining, salaries, affirmative action, performance appraisal, staff welfare, job placement, and career development.

Myers received a master's degree in librarianship from Rutgers University and also holds a master's degree in social work from the University of Illinois. Her bachelor's degree is from Augustana College in Rock Island, Illinois. Prior to coming to the ALA, Myers taught and was placement director at the Rutgers University library school.

This edition has been completely revised by Blythe Camenson. She was educated in Boston, earning her B.A. with a double major in psychology and English from the University of Massachusetts, and her M.Ed. in counseling from Northeastern University. She worked in the mental health field for several years and then moved overseas and taught English as a foreign language in various universities in the Persian Gulf. Now based in Albuquerque, New Mexico, she is a full-time writer and director of Fiction Writer's Connection, a membership organization that helps new writers learn how to get published. Her website is www.fictionwriters.com.

Blythe Camenson has more than four dozen books in print, most published by VGM Career Books, a division of The McGraw-Hill Companies. She is also the co-author of *Your Novel Proposal: From Creation to Contract* (Writer's Digest Books, 1999).

FOREWORD

Ours is an age of information. Each and every day, more and more information becomes available, and the management of this information—from its accumulation to its categorization to its storage to its dissemination—becomes more and more challenging. Imagine manipulating the data not only of days, weeks, or decades past, but of centuries—to the beginning of recorded history and beyond! The task is mammoth, and yet librarians and information professionals do it all the time.

To help people get the variety of information they need quickly and easily, today's librarians and information specialists must be both knowledgeable about where and how to find the desired information and proficient in the ways of accessing it. This means that in many instances they will need prior knowledge about the information being looked for, and they will have to have the expertise necessary to locate it in whatever forms it exists, be it book, tape, microfiche, CD-ROM, journals, the Internet, and so on.

And the choices are many. You can choose to be a generalist or specialist, work with children or doctoral candidates, deal with rare books or musical compilations. The disciplines in which you can work are limited only in the kind and variety of information that exists.

Library and information science is a field that will, obviously, continue to grow and evolve. Consequently, it will need talented, intelligent, innovative, and determined individuals to keep pace with it and to adapt to new ways of managing it. For such individuals, the rewards of this profession are great.

The Editors of VGM Career Books

ACKNOWLEDGMENTS

The authors and editors gratefully acknowledge Peggy Sullivan for her authorship and involvement in previous editions of this work and Kate Lippincott, Research Associate at the University of South Florida, School of Library and Information Science, for research and electronic database searching for this revision.

CHAPTER 1

THE EVOLUTION OF LIBRARIES

The librarian and the information science professional have in common the stewardship of information—its preservation, organization, and dissemination—but the ways that this responsibility is carried out are becoming more and more varied as technology, education, and information expand. Careers in information science and librarianship are based on skills in the organization and retrieval of recorded knowledge. Professionals design and implement systems of categorizing and classifying documents to facilitate their use. The fields of librarianship and information science are expanding rapidly as the computer and communications industries grow more complex.

The variety of career opportunities for the individual educated in the library and information sciences expands every day. Typical careers might be:

- *Information specialist* in the petrochemical industry
- *Director* of a multicounty library system
- *Archivist* in a governmental agency or museum
- *Database searcher* for a nuclear regulatory agency
- *Coordinator* of children's services for an urban library
- *Media specialist* at an elementary or secondary school
- *Systems analyst* for a bibliographic utility
- *Cataloger* of classical language material at an academic library

Any work that requires the organization, analysis, and dissemination of information falls into the domain of the librarian and information scientist.

Traditionally work has been with printed materials, but increasingly these organization skills are applied to electronic, visual, audio, and digital formats. In addition to assembling material, information professionals activate its use for diverse and specialized audiences.

INFORMATION PROFESSIONALS AND WHAT THEY DO

The term *information professional* is broader than either *librarian* or *information scientist* and is used to designate individuals who have been educated to organize, retrieve, and disseminate information. Typically this education consists of a bachelor's degree in the liberal arts or sciences and a master's degree in library and information science. Like education for law, the professional credential for information work builds upon undergraduate specialization. An undergraduate degree in history or literature coupled with the master's degree in library and information science is ideal for public service work in an academic or public library, while an undergraduate degree in biology or chemical engineering coupled with the master's degree in library and information science is appropriate for technical information work in an industrial research center.

Librarians who work with youth (generally called media specialists in elementary or secondary school settings) may have undergraduate preparation in education or social welfare. Those who work with special language collections may have prepared by taking linguistic studies at the undergraduate level. Generally, any undergraduate study complemented with master's-level work in library and information science can be tailored well to a unique specialty.

Information professionals work in every kind of organization. Public institutions such as colleges and universities, public libraries, schools, and government agencies all require individuals skilled in organizing information. Corporations, advertising agencies, trade associations, and nonprofit institutions such as museums and zoos also require the talents of professionals who can manage their records, retrieve data, and assemble facts for analysis.

Salaries of information professionals vary depending upon specialization, geographical region, and the size and type of organization.

While small public libraries may start new graduates with annual salaries in the low twenties, corporate headquarters or pharmaceutical firms often begin salaries in the mid thirties or higher. Directors of large academic libraries or technical information centers can earn more than $100,000 per year. The information professions are so diverse that broad generalizations are difficult. Suffice it to say that individual ability and initiative can result in salary levels comparable to those in any field. See Chapter 4 for additional salary information.

Mobility is great in the information professions. Most positions are advertised nationally, and advancement can take place either within one institution or from one to another. The director of information services at a medium-sized public library can become its director or move on to departmental duties at an urban library. The database searcher at an agricultural library may move on to coordinate on-line information services for a large system. A media specialist at a high school library may become a state consultant for media and instructional technology.

Information professionals are typically affiliated with professional associations such as the American Association of Law Librarians, the American Library Association, the American Society for Information Science, the Medical Library Association, the Society of American Archivists, or the Special Libraries Association. These organizations provide placement services and hold frequent conferences for continuing education.

A HISTORICAL NOTE

The profession of library and information science has strong traditions. The discipline is concerned with the records of culture and thought and should be seen against this background. Perhaps the first individual who had the idea of sorting, collecting, and making more accessible the Mesopotamian clay tablets or Egyptian papyrus scrolls in ancient times should be recognized as the first librarian. By scanning many centuries, we can see that the status of the librarian—that is, the person responsible for maintaining a collection of information materials for use by others—rose when the need for records was recognized as important. The librarian was probably first seen as an organizer of materials—not books as we know them today—but, rather, bulky rolls or tablets that had to be preserved if they were to be useful to others.

The Middle Ages

The values of the materials varied at different times also because of their relative availability. For example, in the Middle Ages, when links with earlier cultures were few, the people concerned with records preservation attached an exceptionally great value to their work. Today their work remains essential to our understanding of those early times, although it still has received little recognition. The determination and the development of skills for the preservation of materials still are significant in the work of librarians.

Centuries before anyone dreamed of special education for librarians, it was customary for leaders of church and state to appoint a few well-read, well-organized individuals to collect materials and arrange them so that the leaders and their colleagues could find what they wanted. These individuals were probably the first people who consciously thought of themselves as librarians. In almost every Indo-European language, the words for *library* and *librarian* are closely related to those for *books*. In French, Danish, German, and other European languages, the syllable *biblio* is found in words for libraries and librarians. The same letter combination appears in ancient terms for books and in such English words as *bibliography* and *Bible*. The English word, *librarian,* derives from the Latin word for book, *liber.* In many languages, the term designating the people who work with these materials is very similar to the term for the materials themselves.

The 1600s and 1700s

In the mid-1600s, Gabriel Naudé, librarian to Cardinal Mazarin of France, wrote his now-famous book, *Advice on Establishing a Library,* as a practical guide for others to use in organizing collections of materials and encouraging their use. He may be considered the first known professional librarian.

Libraries became more essential as universities and colleges developed. The technological development of printing had encouraged the proliferation of new works and new copies of materials, and the number of literate people increased. Their subsequent gathering in universities virtually required the development of a way for them to share their materials and to make knowledge more readily available to students. Faculties—usually a group of scholars studying in the same general area—shared their information materials and selected someone, often one of themselves, to be responsible for this new collection. This individual also was to consult them about adding to the collection and to offer such appropriate services as might be required. Depending on the size, tradition, and other characteristics of the university, it sometimes seemed reasonable to combine these collections into larger, more general collections. This could make accessibility of the information more equitable and provide a program of general services.

The 1800s and Early 1900s

Early libraries in the United States, although they functioned as public libraries, were often limited in the publics they served. Apprentices, members of a certain society, or students in a Sunday school might be the major audience for whom a library existed.

One of the most long-lasting benefits to public libraries was the series of grants made for public library building by Andrew Carnegie and the Carnegie Corporation in the late 1800s and early 1900s. Each community had to promise to maintain its library, but the prospect of receiving such funds encouraged many communities to plan public library service.

Public libraries were important in the task of helping the many immigrants who came to this country in the 1800s and early 1900s to become a part of American society. There were special problems in working with people whose language and background differed from those of their neighbors, but public libraries attempted to serve them. They reached parents through their children and expanded the library's traditional schedule to provide times when the immigrants, who often worked long hours, could come to the library. Expanded collections of foreign language materials and programs that provided citizenship classes also were important features of this effort.

In the last quarter of the 1800s, two developments helped to change the character of libraries and librarians. A key figure in both was Melvil

Dewey; he developed the Dewey Decimal Classification, used in many libraries today, and he was the vocal leader in the founding of the American Library Association and in the establishment of a formal educational program for librarians. Both of these developments were significant for the professionalization of librarianship. Librarians came to know each other through annual American Library Association (ALA) conferences. Through shared experiences and formal discussions, they began to express themselves as a group on such issues as library cooperation and development, public relations, censorship, copyright policy and law, and library management.

Dewey's school, first located at Columbia College and later at Albany, New York, provided an opportunity for librarians to prepare themselves with a formal course of study. They learned classification, binding of books, and use of reference materials, as well as library history. Other schools, at universities or colleges and public libraries, were founded in the first quarter of the 1900s. Then, in response to recognition given to librarianship as a profession and the need for standardization of library education, the American Library Association recommended that library education programs be established only in institutions of higher learning.

If higher scholarship demanded access to more materials, there was no such tradition in lower-level schools until much later. *Blab schools,* so named from the practice of having children recite out loud, heavily emphasized memory usage and made little use of such scarce and expensive learning materials as books. Obviously, they were hardly places where libraries were likely to be established. Blab schools existed throughout the United States until well within the last hundred years.

Early in the 1900s, the push for libraries in elementary and secondary schools began with the recognition that high school students and faculties required organized resource materials. Once established, library use had to be encouraged, so dynamic high school libraries developed. Elementary schools have a shorter history, coming to the fore primarily after World War II. School library media specialists often came from the ranks of teachers, although the number of school libraries and the need for librarians in recent years have encouraged more people to train for this specialty as a first career. Today most U.S. school systems employ full-time media specialists.

As the profession matured, special libraries developed. Special libraries are often associated with particular industries or businesses; but collections of special materials such as maps or special subjects such as art often form special libraries, too.

The Special Libraries Association, founded in the first decade of the 1900s, fosters the continuing education of its members and assistance in development of techniques for greater service and efficiency. Special librarians are located in major population centers, like Chicago, Washington, D.C., or Boston, as well as in research centers, corporate headquarters, and research and development laboratories throughout the world.

DEVELOPMENT OF INFORMATION SCIENCE

The field of *information science,* which has grown rapidly during the past fifty years, is closely allied to library science. The American Society for Information Science (ASIS), founded in 1937, is an association whose diverse membership continues to reflect the frontiers and horizons of the dynamic field of information science and technology.

The information profession is concerned with the ways people create, collect, organize, store, retrieve, send, analyze, and use information. The subject discipline that forms the basis for this field is called *information science,* the study of the characteristics of information and how it is transferred or handled. The field of information science emerged in the 1950s from several other disciplines, including computer science, library science, communications, business administration, mathematics, engineering, psychology, philosophy, and language arts. Information science emphasizes the application of modern technologies—joining together processes and systems, computers, satellites and other technologies, and human resources—to provide information and information services.

Those who work to disseminate information in a variety of formats, whether they ally themselves with library associations or information associations, aim at a common goal of getting information to people who need it. What stands out about the library and information field is the diversity of the types of work and the locations in which this work is carried on.

The history of information agencies is closely tied to technological developments. The activities of the information professions have always been closely associated with technological advances. A suggestion made by the librarian at the surgeon general's office led to the development of mechanical card sorters, the predecessors of today's computers. The development of microfilm was a response to the need to store large amounts of textual information. Libraries and other information agencies were among the first large-scale users of computers, and many advances in the use and design of computer systems have come about as a result of the needs of libraries and information centers. Some of today's most challenging problems of computer programming and computer systems design are related to the needs of libraries and information systems.

LIBRARIES TODAY

Librarians and information science professionals face important, exciting challenges and a broad array of opportunities. By examining some of the key roles of the library as identified by the American Library Association, it is possible to gain a sense of the scope:

Librarians and information professionals activate the resources of the library so that citizens can make informed decisions.   A democracy requires the active participation of its citizenry, and libraries play a vital role in making knowledge and ideas available to everyone. The relationship of democracy and libraries is fundamental, and the stronger the library services are, the more powerful citizens' voices will be.

Libraries break down barriers.   Literacy outreach programs that teach reading, provide bilingual materials, serve the homebound, and work with the elderly continue to be a priority for librarians in order to reach parts of the population that others are failing to reach. The barriers to those who are illiterate, low-literate, and non-English-speaking are enormous, and the loss to society as a whole can have far-reaching effects.

Libraries level the playing field.   As the income inequities in this country grow, the library is one public institution that provides equality of information to all. As technology and the Internet converge, the need for librarians and information professionals to provide equity to information becomes crucial.

Libraries value the individual. For many authors, scientists, and politicians a librarian provided the encouragement and support needed to learn and grow. Testimonies from many successful citizens credit librarians and information professionals with opening the door to the storehouse of the world's knowledge.

Libraries nourish creativity. Librarians and information professionals will make it possible for learners to gain access to the books, web pages, and digitized collections that lead to new scholarship, poetry, and scientific achievement.

Libraries open children's minds. Story hours for preschoolers, stories told with wonder and magic, support for schoolwork, and individualized attention by librarians provide expansion of the world to young minds.

Libraries return high dividends. Economic development for the small business and other community enterprises is found through the collaboration with librarians and other information professionals to assist in the development of business plans, the collection of data for public relations and marketing, and other crucial resources for business development.

Libraries build communities. Meeting rooms at libraries provide a chance for communities to gather together and learn from one another. Librarians provide support to groups as diverse as investors and clowns. Together the community and the staff of library and information professionals make a world where people care about each other and their future.

Libraries make families friendlier. Librarians support families in learning together through home schooling support, story hours, support for science projects, and intergenerational reading programs.

Libraries make people think. Librarians work to balance opinions and ideas within the collections they maintain. Challenges to old ways and ideas that make us think are brought together by the thoughtful work of librarians and information professionals who gather together collections for the community to read and ponder.

Libraries offer sanctuary. Librarians ensure that the wise words of scholars and scientists and artists from the past are available in a manner that is accessible to all.

Libraries preserve the past. Librarians sift through the onslaught of media to save and preserve our cultural heritage. In addition to its selection, the preservation of this heritage, whether archival or digital, is the role of the librarians.

These roles of libraries appeared in the December 1995 issue of the official journal of the American Library Association, *American Libraries*. Although these roles are timeless, their implementation will change in the future.

NUMBER OF LIBRARIES IN THE UNITED STATES

The American Library Association estimates that there are 122,289 libraries of all kinds in the United States today. No annual survey provides statistics on all types of libraries. The counts listed below for public, academic, and school libraries come from the most recent versions of three different surveys by the National Center for Education Statistics (NCES). Figures for special libraries, armed forces libraries, and government libraries are provided by the *American Library Directory 2000–2001,* compiled by the R. R. Bowker company.

Public Libraries—Administrative Units		8,967
(Central buildings	8,943)	
(Branches	7,147)	
(Buildings	16,090)	
Academic Libraries		3,408
Less than four-year	1,293	
Four year and above	2,115	

School Libraries		98,169
Public schools	77,218	
Private schools	20,951	
*Special Libraries**		9,993
Armed Forces Libraries		*341*
Government Libraries		*1,411*
Total		**122,289**

* Libraries considered "special libraries" are those with a particular focus such as: corporate, law, medical, religious, etc.

CHAPTER 2

INFORMATION PROFESSIONALS ON THE JOB

Where are today's information professionals working? Although more and more might exclaim, "cyberspace!" the new information professionals are still likely to be affiliated with an institution. What are their institutions like? If we think of libraries as buildings, we may envision a new academic library, containing acres of space and rare manuscripts. Yet the university's library system may include departmental libraries managed by a small staff, with many services performed by the central library. The degree of that departmental librarian's independence from the library system may vary, but the point is that both the departmental librarian and the librarian in the large central library are working for the same system. Thus, while departmental librarians may exercise very special skills in the management of a Slavic literature collection or a Far Eastern studies collection, they are usually tied to the central library through common governance, computer systems, and centralized processing.

Similarly, in a public library system, there may be librarians in a downtown central library whose work is highly specialized in the kinds of assistance they provide to users, such as business information, literacy education, exhibits development, or humanities programming. In the same system's neighborhood branch libraries, a small staff may deal with all ages and kinds of readers and coordinate programs with community organizations and schools.

However, many information professionals, especially those in corporate or research institutes, focus on the retrieval of information from databases thousands of miles away from their offices. Legal or medical information loaded into large databases by vendors can be reached through computer terminals and searched for highly discrete facts. Manipulation of numeric or full-text databases by information professionals results in raw source material for corporate planning or scientific discoveries.

Some information professionals offer their services for a fee to clients and work independently as information brokers or have joined the growing numbers of companies that create and market information. There are thousands of companies that employ information specialists to provide primary and secondary information, custom search computer and manual sources, and provide information-support services.

Health science libraries employ professionals to develop collections, educate medical staff in medical informatics, and coordinate electronic resources access. A hospital librarian may serve as a member of a healthcare team or participate in patient education.

Bookmobiles are another place of employment for information professionals. Usually bookmobiles are associated with rural areas, where they bring books to isolated locations. They may also have routes that include urban shopping centers or city neighborhoods and suburbs, where access to other library agencies is too difficult for many people. Some school systems provide bookmobile service to small schools that cannot employ a media specialist on a regular basis. Because bookmobiles can be moved, they often are used to demonstrate the resources of a community's library at events that may reach new segments of a community, like a city arts festival or a county fair.

Examples of special libraries of corporations are Motorola, Mead Data Central, or pharmaceutical groups. Newspapers employ on-line data searchers, photo archivists, and web masters. Museum libraries hire information professionals to organize archives, catalogs, and research collections.

A special library may occupy a suite of offices in a corporation's headquarters. It also may occupy smaller areas in various regional offices, just as a library serving a sprawling research institute may have several different units located nearest the areas where they are most relevant.

Law libraries are employed by legal firms and university libraries. These information professionals are astute at searching multiple databases for case law and precedent. Great strides in library cooperation have been made since the 1960s. Large regional libraries or systems employ consultant librarians who work with individual libraries in their areas to foster exchange of library materials, cooperative cataloging and acquisition, and electronic systems coordination.

RESPONSIBILITIES OF INFORMATION PROFESSIONALS

If the locations of information employment vary so much, does the work that makes up the information professional's day differ to the same degree? Three examples suggest that the work shows even more variety. Yet there are also similarities in the kinds of responsibilities and concerns that are part of the work of three very different kinds of information professionals.

Information Brokers

Lee Fox and Mary Raney met while graduate students in an information science program and decided to set up their own "information-on-demand" business upon graduation. On a typical morning, Fox stops at a government library to peruse legal reports for a client involved in personal injury litigation, while Raney goes directly to their office to conduct a computer search of environmental regulations for a firm that is seeking a municipal permit to develop a landfill.

Their secretary notifies them that an emergency call has come through from a small financial counseling firm that needs a search of the ABI/Inform database to assist a new account. While the computer runs off environmental data, Raney calls up the financial database to begin that search.

When Fox returns from the library with a list of legal citations, he passes them on to their word processing operator and begins to analyze census data from Standard Metropolitan Statistical Area (SMSA) block statistics to assist another client who needs marketing data.

Throughout their day, Lee and Mary use printed and computer sources to retrieve and compile information needed by their many clients. Initially they billed $50 per hour for services, but their client load has become so large that they now have a list of those for whom they work on a contingency basis. The expense for each of these clients is greatly decreased by the use of skilled information brokers rather than full-time employment of a staff specialist.

Public Library Director

The director of one county public library with twenty-seven neighborhood branches probably begins the day by a careful, although hurried, reading of the daily newspaper. The director needs to know what the county commission candidates are promising to voters, what prospects are for new industries, whether zoning law changes may affect residential areas and the location of branch libraries, and any other information about the county that may affect the library and the public it serves.

On the national scene, the director will be interested in legislation relating to telecommunications and to libraries, news of controversies elsewhere about library materials, and general information about the economy. She will likely correspond with members of Congress on legislation relating to library funding.

Later in the morning, the director may attend at least a portion of a meeting of young adult librarians. This provides an opportunity to get acquainted with staff members from outlying neighborhood branches who may come to the central library only a few times a year.

The director's other morning appointments may include the library's legal counsel, who is reporting on a case instigated by an employee injured on duty. The director may meet with the architect to review plans for renovation of one of the older branch libraries and later ask the human resources department to inform her about progress in filling a position to be vacated by an important staff member who is retiring soon. A staff committee, working with the human resources department, may have much of the responsibility for that appointment, but the director will want to be informed of their criteria and their scheduling of interviews. The director may participate in those interviews or schedule a separate one with some candidates, especially if the position is an important one in the library system.

Lunch, which might be a respite from the several meetings, is more likely to be an extension of them. The director may be invited to lunch with a community organization that is requesting expansion of the Asian-language collection for new citizens or with a committee from the school board seeking to create homework centers in partnership with neighborhood branches.

In the afternoon, the director may spend several hours away from the library to meet with other county department heads to consider reductions to the county's proposed budget. At this meeting the director may argue the need for investment in a regional cooperative library system, which will benefit the county's own library system.

At the end of the working day, the director may read correspondence that includes a request to serve on the state library task force on networking, a request from a social services agency about the need for a job center at a branch library, a letter from a former colleague recommending an applicant for an open position, and a questionnaire from a federal agency about the library's services to the aging—just to name a few of the many responsibilities. The director may then dictate some answers.

The end of the day finds the director heading home, briefcase full of annual departmental reports and professional journals that must be read to keep up with the latest developments in technology. That evening the director attends a civic meeting where discussion is scheduled on a new facility that would serve as community clinic, day-care center, and library.

University Library Director

The day of a library director at a university has some similarities to that of the public library director. This director, too, needs to know the current concerns of the public, to meet with university vice presidents and deans to discuss the budget, to be alert to various specialists' interests on the library staff, and to deal with a range of problems relating to the need for more storage space, new copyright laws, the cost of electronic reference services, and so on.

The academic library director's correspondence may be similar to the public library director's in amount and kind. The social obligations— perhaps attending a lecture by a professor of comparative literature who has just donated valuable manuscripts to the library's special collections—would also have similarities.

Since scholarship is often an important aspect of academic librarianship, the director may spend an hour developing notes for a journal article about the cost-effectiveness of computerized acquisitions systems or evaluating the publication record of a staff member who is being considered for promotion.

Both directors probably started out in librarianship thinking that they wanted to work with books and with people. At the administrative level the work of these professionals is primarily organizing, planning, and representing.

SPECIALIZATION OF WORK
BY TYPE OF INSTITUTION

Although many categories of institutions may be discussed, the main ones are public libraries, special libraries, academic libraries, school library media centers, and other information agencies. Within each category there are positions that are quite similar to positions elsewhere, and an individual may move without difficulty from one type to another.

Public Libraries

Probably most familiar are public libraries. These are supported by public monies, which come from the local community, the county, the state, the federal government, or some mix of these agencies. Although private funds such as endowments may supplement the funding, public libraries are likely to be closely tied to the economic situation of government support. Another major characteristic is that their programs and priorities usually are based on the general needs of the public as a whole.

In structure, it is more and more common for public libraries to be linked with others in some administrative pattern. Some systems stem from a strong central library providing services to numerous smaller branch libraries. Others are composed of a number of independent or fairly independent libraries that have combined to share resources more effectively but that have considerable administrative freedom. Since the nature of the structure can have considerable effect on the individual working in any one of the libraries, it is a good idea for any prospective employee to learn about the structure before applying for and certainly before accepting a position in a public library.

Public library services may extend considerably beyond the public library buildings, which are clearly visible. Bookmobile service as well as service to jails, retirement homes, institutions for the mentally ill, and other similar places often are provided by the public library on a regular basis or in special programs.

Special Libraries and Information Centers

Special libraries and information centers may be subdivided into many categories, including medical, legal, hospital, commercial, and industrial. Their audience is usually carefully defined—the research staff of a chemical corporation, scholars who wish to use the library of a museum or art gallery, or patients of a hospital. An important distinction should be made, incidentally, between medical and hospital libraries. The former usually are comprised of special collections of medical books and other media required by researchers and practitioners in a hospital, medical school, or similar institution; the latter are more like general libraries in the scope of their collections and are used by hospital patients, staff, and visitors. Medical librarians need background and information about medicine as a field of study. Hospital librarians provide more general materials, so that, while information about various patients' attitudes and disabilities may be useful, they do not always need the specific background in medical sources.

There is a growing trend for agencies that have special libraries in various branch offices or regional headquarters to build them into networks for greater efficiency. Thus, a producer of agricultural equipment may have a library at its main midwestern plant that includes materials on engineering, patents, and aspects of production and inventory control, while another information center in its corporate headquarters may provide information about marketing, advertising, legal questions, and other matters that concern that staff. Yet it may be useful for each library to know about the work and the content of the other. This trend often results in computerized data banks, electronic communication, or exchange of personnel. Therefore, special libraries that may appear small in some aspects may, in reality, offer great diversity of experience and complexity of management.

Special libraries, which are not usually tied directly to the public economy, may offer more prospect of expansion than other kinds of libraries. The services that special library staffs provide their clientele—journal routing in specialized fields, new publications and productions awareness services, clipping services, quick reference, abstracts, web pages, or bibliographic searches—offer suggestions for those interested in developing freelance library and information services that will be valuable to others.

In many instances it is hard to draw a sharp line between special librarians and information scientists. Even more than other librarians, special librarians may be concerned with providing a direct link with the information sought, not referring the requester to another library or information agency. As noted earlier, they also are likely to have a close link of interest and competence with the subject field. Law libraries, for instance, often are headed by lawyers who later became librarians or by librarians who have some legal knowledge.

Academic Libraries

All accredited institutions of higher education in the United States have libraries. The library, since it exists to serve the goals of the institution, may be highly oriented to research or more directed to the information needs of students or some combination of the two. Major growth in the establishment of community colleges in the 1960s included development of library programs that incorporated many kinds of media, were usually planned with the needs of the adult learner in mind, and provided extended hours and locations of services to accommodate the schedules and sprawling campuses of the institutions.

Library programs in four-year colleges range in diversity as much as the colleges do in their programs, locations, and goals. These libraries also may be small, but because of the recognized value of cooperation among libraries, many have, in recent years, formed formal or informal networks to make interlibrary loans, union lists of serials, and collection development more efficient.

University libraries tend to be more concerned with research than other academic libraries. This means that acquiring and providing access to a large and richly varied collection of library materials are of great importance. Services provided to students, faculty members, and researchers call for library personnel who have enough knowledge of subject areas in which advanced degrees are offered.

Academic librarians are often very involved with teaching. Government reports on education have underscored the need for Americans to become adept at information use, and academic librarians specialize in classes that teach skills to students at all levels. Many academic libraries have implemented faculty seminars and student seminars in the use of information resources, often focusing on electronic access.

Academic libraries, especially those serving large universities, are the repositories of many rare and specialized collections. Work in these collections may require extensive and specialized subject expertise on the part of employees. Government documents from Southeast Asia, oral histories of Native Americans, manuscript collections of public officials, and rare art prints and engravings are just a few of the types of materials collected in academic libraries that employ subject experts.

School Library Media Centers

On the whole, the development of school library media centers in the United States is relatively recent. Earlier service to schools from state education agencies or from public libraries has yielded to provisions for media centers within each school. In most school systems the tradition of library service is usually older at the secondary level than at the elementary level. At both levels emphasis usually is placed on provision of materials and services that are closely related to the school's curriculum. In recent years the move toward provision of a range of instructional technology, CD-ROM, and hypermedia—films, videotapes, recordings, and graphic materials—has been strong in school library media centers. Today, Internet access and the provision of computers have made media specialists among the most technically expert in school systems.

The close relation of the school library media center to the curriculum usually results in the media specialist teaching, especially in the areas of research and use of instructional technology. As teaching information retrieval skills is a central responsibility, there are many occasions when the school library media specialist conducts classes. Teaching skill is expected in school media personnel, and most who enter this specialization have come from the ranks of teachers.

School system library services may be more complex than those of public libraries, with technical services, networking and instructional technology, film loans, professional libraries for teachers, and other related services offered by system headquarters. Supervisors of such programs may evaluate the work of media specialists in individual schools and also be responsible for providing services from the system.

It would be misleading to leave the impression that all school library media centers are in public schools and that all are parts of systems. Private, parochial, and other nonpublic schools share many characteristics of the school library media centers described, but each school tends to be more independent in setting its own program and priorities than is a public school within a system. These schools also are less likely to have such specific requirements about certification of personnel.

Certification is usually required of all teaching and administrative personnel in school systems. Librarians and media specialists may be required to hold certification in those specialties and to have certification as teachers. Although requirements vary from one state to another, since certification is administered by state education agencies, there are some common patterns. Academic work in education, with courses in teaching methods, psychology, the organization of schools, and related subjects, is usually a requirement. The individual also is usually expected to provide some evidence of competence, either as a student teacher, media intern, or perhaps a regularly employed teacher or librarian, which shows he or she has worked well in a situation similar to the one for which he or she will receive a certificate.

Because of the problems for individuals who move from one state to another and need to fulfill differing requirements, and because of the problems of administering certification programs, many states have made reciprocity agreements to accept each other's certificates. A person with a teaching, library, or media certificate in one state may be eligible for certification in another state simply by presenting proof of previous certification. No assumptions should be made about certification, however, because programs change. What is important is to realize the significance of certification in employment in a school system and to take action to achieve it.

Other Information Agencies

So far we have discussed library and information employment along the lines of four major categories of institutions: public libraries, special libraries, academic libraries, and school library media centers. We have also seen, from the example of information brokers, that some professionals in this field are not tied to specific institutions at all in order to earn a living.

Many government agencies at the federal, state, or international level require the services of information professionals or consultants. The U.S. Congress or a state legislature, for instance, needs analysis of laws and precedents for its deliberations on public policy; an information analysis center such as the Oak Ridge National Laboratory requires organization of research, reports, regulations, and environmental impact studies; a national opinion research center must have its data tapes stored and organized for access. These varied agencies employ individuals who are competent in organization skills. As the nation's output of information steadily increases, professional positions will expand in such areas.

SPECIALIZATION BY PROFESSIONAL FUNCTION

Although many information professionals can characterize their work by type of institution—as "academic librarians" or "information institute analysts"—there are many, many types of positions in each institution. We will describe some of the primary functional job types in order to demonstrate the kinds of work that information professionals do within institutions that serve very different publics.

Public Service

The object of most information-related work is service to a public, although that public may be defined in different ways. The challenge of the search for information and of dealing with a public that may know exactly what it wants but is unable or unwilling to express it are the twin challenges that attract people to public service in the information professions. Yet, even they—the children's librarian who may have a lively preschool story hour in the morning and a hectic two hours of reference assistance in the afternoon; the librarian who divides her or his time between assisting patrons at the on-line catalog and working at the telephone information desk; the bookmobile librarian who stands while assisting eager users at two three-hour stops during the day—have behind-the-scenes work that must be done. The children's librarian must prepare a budget to provide for the rebinding of the many books that were new when the library opened and that have, therefore, all worn out at the same time. The reference librarian needs to scan review journals to select items for purchase, and the bookmobile librarian may spend time between stops catching up on the work of choosing new books. These are only a few of the tasks they need to do, and yet each of these people would be classed as a public service librarian. Some varieties of public service work are discussed on the following pages.

Information Services There are several levels of information service provided in libraries and related agencies. These include "ready reference," often by telephone or E-mail; basic assistance in answering complicated questions requiring several sources; and in-depth assistance.

Ready reference queries include such questions as: "Who won the 2000 Nobel Peace Prize?" "What are the major novels of the author Manlio Argueta?" "Is the boiling point of mercury higher than that of bauxite?" "How many votes did Bill Clinton receive the second time he ran for president?" Academic, public, or community college librarians who provide this service may use common reference sources such as almanacs or encyclopedias to respond, but they increasingly are turning to electronic reference tools or the Internet.

The second level of information assistance may require several sources for an adequate answer. Examples include such questions as, "Can you help me identify key arguments on the abortion issue?" or "How have architects integrated ideas from modern art into their building facades?"

In research libraries or special libraries serving a demanding clientele, information professionals do more than advise on answers or sources. They execute on-line computer searches, retrieve cited documents, and even analyze their contents. At a law library, for instance, a legal scholar may need to prepare a paper on the validity of the pay equity argument. In response to this need the law librarian may search databases such as LEXIS, then copy relevant citations from microformatted sources, and finally prepare a legislative history of pertinent laws.

In a health sciences library, the medical librarian asked to assist a surgeon on a cancer case will most likely search CANCERLIT on-line, MEDLARS, or even EIS (Digest of Environmental Impact Statements) to collect all relevant documents. On-line searching provides quick and comprehensive data for the skilled searcher to apply to the problem at hand.

Closely allied to information services is the interlibrary or cooperative function. The capacity to search hundreds of electronic databases for bibliographic citations or full text creates a greater demand for the original sources. If the library does not hold these sources, then the information services librarian will need to access a computerized or manual listing of the serial or monographic holdings of other research collections to initiate document retrieval.

Information and Referral   Closely allied to information services is the information and referral (or I & R) function. I & R centers, usually housed in public libraries or governmental agencies, put people together with resources that meet their needs for survival. An unemployed laborer whose child is in need of diabetic counseling can contact the I & R service to discover if there are any publically provided health counseling clinics. A retired grocer whose social security check has been stolen can contact the I & R service for information on the right course of action. Often I & R professionals have undergraduate preparation in social welfare in addition to graduate study in library and information science.

Readers' Services   There is no single good term for the kinds of assistance provided in general readers' services. In the 1940s, public libraries placed heavy emphasis on guidance of readers, suggesting individually designed reading programs for enjoyment or educational value. Librarians who provided this kind of service were usually called readers' advisers. The term is used less often today, but the service has continued and, in some libraries, has expanded considerably. Although some libraries have continued the more personalized service, many others provide as much assistance as possible through "floor work" by staff members. Conversational guidance and assistance may be conducted in a very informal way, but the purpose usually is to provide as much assistance as is available and useful to the library user.

Many of a library's services may result from observations made by those providing readers' services. Repeated inquiries about income tax information, for example, may make it clear that the collection on that topic needs to be considerably expanded or that a series of talks by accountants or representatives of the Internal Revenue Service would be a worthwhile public service for the library to provide. The observant librarian who provides readers' services in an academic library may realize the need to start a program of library skills instruction if many users seem unable to locate what they want on their own.

Although most of readers' services work will involve direct communication with the public, the work can be extended effectively through many other channels. Providing bulletin boards for events within the school, college, or community is one example. Other exhibits designed to increase public awareness of the library's services and programs, such as a local history corner to point out extensive genealogical resources, are also a logical part of the service provided to readers.

Service Provided to People in Special Categories   These types of services usually have developed from a library's readers' services programs. Categories by age are common enough in public libraries, for example. Service to children probably has the longest tradition in this country. In recent years, service to the aging also has been recognized as an important area. Those who work with these age groups need to know what materials are available as well as have an understanding of the particular characteristics of each age group. But even understanding is not enough; respect for the individual, in spite of the possible discipline problems that children may create or the querulousness of the senile, is essential.

Special librarians, including those who may be in such departments as science and technology in a public or academic library, also have a public selected for them to some extent, since their collections attract a certain kind of user. This is true for several other specialties. Other assignments in which one part of the public is designated as a librarian's responsibility may be ones where all of the homebound people in a community request library service through one librarian, who conducts an active telephone service and schedules deliveries by volunteers or other staff members. Service to the blind and people with other disabilities also may be specifically assigned to one person or to a team whose skills are appropriate to that work.

There are many more examples of public service specialization for certain groups. In large urban areas librarians with fluency in the dominant languages of various ethnic communities may be in demand to provide public services or to tell stories to children. Prison library service usually requires an individual with some social service background who has skills in coping with the special problems of those who are institutionalized. Librarians in rural county libraries would best serve their agricultural publics with some background in the information needs of the farming community. Information professionals who choose these specific types of publics with which to work generally supplement their general library skills with continuing education in order to provide better service, if they do not come to these positions with previous background.

Other Aspects of Public Service   It should be clear from this discussion that there are a number of kinds of public service, and some positions cut across other categories to include public service as part of their responsibilities. Also, many members of library and information center staffs who think of their work or specialization as being a subject (art and chemistry) or a format of media (films or musical recordings) are really important members of the public service staff. Bookmobile staff members obviously are, as are those who provide service to the homebound, give book talks or storytelling programs in schools or at camps, or are on call or provide programs for adult service clubs and similar groups.

Technical Services

The effectiveness of public service personnel is no better than the quality of work that makes their service possible. To cite an obvious example, it would be meaningless for a museum's librarian to offer to display good books available for Christmas purchases if the books had not been ordered, organized or cataloged, and delivered to the museum library's exhibition cases for display.

Librarians who make these services possible usually are described as technical services personnel. The increasing complexity of the types of materials published and the changing technologies used to catalog and classify material have meant that the once-distinct lines between public and technical librarians have blurred. In the largest sense, technical services librarians provide much public service. Types of technical services specialization are described below.

Acquisitions   Librarians in acquisitions work have the responsibility for deciding which items a library will purchase, the agent from whom they will be purchased (an increasingly complex task as vendors of books computerize their operations), and how the library will coordinate all the suggestions it receives about purchases. Such work may require extremely specialized knowledge about the book trade, especially when foreign materials make up a sizable portion of the collection, as well as a keen understanding of the public for whom the materials are selected. The librarian who acquires college-level materials for a community where the reading level is low fails to respond adequately to that community. It is clear that the acquisitions librarian must learn much about the local constituency before ordering material for the library at hand.

Prior to ordering material, the acquisition librarian often reads several reviews of a single item from a variety of professional journals to ascertain the item's value to the library. Careful records must be kept in order to avoid duplication and to ensure that information is available to allow efficient cataloging and classification of items to be added to the collection. Today much acquisition work is done through computerized systems that maintain machine-readable files of a given library's holdings. Vendors can be notified via telecommunications of new orders. Skill in the use of these automated systems is now fundamental to the acquisitions process.

Many libraries now are hiring collection development or collection management librarians to provide oversight in shaping and building the collection and in directing the growth of the collection to meet the needs of the library's public.

Cataloging   This is the process of describing library material so that users will know whether they wish to see it. Most libraries now are using computerized catalogs that permit users to search by author, title, subject, or keyword. Unless we use libraries in some very sophisticated way or for some particular purpose, we may not realize all the decisions necessary to make the catalog as useful as it can be. A cataloger needs to make decisions based on a whole range of questions, of which these are only a few:

- Are people more likely to look for Victoria Holt's books under that name or under one of the same writer's several pseudonyms? Will users want to know that the same writer is Jean Plaidy, for example?
- Since studies show that most university students want the most recent title on a subject, should we consider rearranging much of our catalog, with the titles that are on the same subject arranged by publication date, rather than by author?
- Is acupuncture so significant—and does the library have enough books on the topic—that it should have a subject heading?
- Will third-graders be able to find books on the sea if the heading for them is OCEANOGRAPHY? If not, what shall we do?
- In a set of four filmstrips, is it important for the user to know the title of each, or is the title of the set enough?

- If we have a backlog of materials to be cataloged, how can we decide which groups of materials should have priority?

The list of questions could be much longer, but the point is to suggest the range of the cataloger's concerns and to indicate how closely they are related to those of public service librarians and to the library's users. It is also clear that the cataloger's decisions involve other members of the library staff, including the budget officer and administrators, who must decide whether such decisions are feasible.

Because catalogers deal primarily with the library's materials, they may need such skills as special knowledge in various subject areas, reading knowledge of one or more foreign languages, and ability to skim reading materials rapidly to decide how they should be organized. Skills concerning such nonprint materials as films, recordings, photographic slides, or videotapes and computer software are still different, possibly requiring a knowledge of music, ability to identify artists and composers when their names do not appear on the material, and a variety of other abilities. Within this one specialty of cataloging there may be many other specializations, such as music, law, serials, and government documents; in large collections the catalogers will have to be especially adept at handling the many special items that are part of the library. And, while a sense of how the readers will use a collection is important for catalogers to have, they need to make decisions in isolation, without opportunity to refer to the practices in other libraries or to ask for several options. They need to have competence and assurance about their own judgments. There is something fascinating about sorting and putting together similar things and separating different things. Catalogers thrive on that fascination.

Cataloging information can come from a number of different sources. These include the Library of Congress, networks or consortia such as the On-line Computer Library Center (OCLC), the Research Libraries Information Network (RLIN), and the Western Library Network (WLN).

Although the availability of cataloging data from external sources has made it possible for libraries to assign many cataloging tasks to support staff, there is always some need for original cataloging. Professional catalogers generally are responsible for cataloging items for which no external sources of data are available and for supervising the activities of support staff.

Cataloging requires the ability to understand rapidly the general theme and content of the material to be cataloged. Attention to detail, an important characteristic of catalogers, requires that they verify much information and make the material they are adding to the library's collection as accessible as possible. Is the book really a second edition? Does the library already have a copy of the recording? How can the discussion guide that accompanies a film be made as accessible as the film? These questions are important to consider and answer.

Intellectual ability, possibly including the ability to read several foreign languages, is important for a cataloger. The assignment of a classification number, often the only task an outsider is aware of, may be the smallest and least important part of the cataloger's duties.

There is a need for constant exercise of judgment and understanding of what characteristics may be traded off for others in the whole area of technical services. Is it, for example, so important to get large quantities of seasonal materials to the patrons that they can be processed with only a minimal amount of cataloging information noted? Should paperback books on various careers be prepared so that they can be filed in a vertical file by subject, rather than listed in a card catalog by author, title, and subject? Should terms that have become dated or misleading because of changed usage be dropped as subject headings—SCIENCE FICTION replacing INTERPLANETARY VOYAGES—FICTION, for instance? If so, should all earlier items also have their headings changed? These examples merely suggest the responsibilities of the cataloger, which are usually shared with the head of technical services.

Other Technical Processes   The behind-the-scenes processing of library materials does not end with the cataloging and classification of materials. A wide variety of other processing activities also must take place. Materials must be marked so that they can be properly placed within the collection, and the process of preparing materials for circulation may require preparing the materials themselves and preparing records for a manual or automated circulation system. Many materials require special treatment: audiovisual media, computer software, archival materials, pamphlets, and rare books all must be handled with special care. Although the processes themselves may be routine, the decisions made regarding those processes require careful professional attention, and new methods and techniques will need to be developed and instituted as changes take place in needs and materials. Technical services librarians are often on the cutting edge of library technology.

Technical services also may include provision of such processes as mending of materials, binding, and the referral of some items to an outside agency for repair. It may be that a film department, for instance, will attach its own leader (a blank strip similar to the film itself used at the beginning of the film, sometimes with a notation as to the title and owner of the copy), or this chore may be a part of technical services. Reinforcing paperbacks within the technical services department may prove to be more economical than paying the increased price for ones reinforced by the supplier. And it may make a lot of sense for the technical services staff to have the responsibility for gathering up all serials and journals to be bound, keeping a record of what is sent, and handling all the physical aspects of that work.

In fact with many libraries spending an increasing amount of their resources on periodicals and journals, and with the growing numbers of these items available, periodicals or serials work is becoming a specialty in technical processes. Preservation activities also are of increasing importance, to protect and prolong the life of the collection.

Library and Information System Automation   Some of the first practical uses of computers were made in libraries, and automation has had a pervasive effect on the information professions. Computers are used for everything from teaching tools in school library media centers to computer-managed archives in corporate information centers to huge systems of multidisciplinary databases provided by search service vendors. Although automation was at first limited to large institutions with substantial budgets, advancing technology has made the adoption of computer technology feasible even for very small public and school libraries. This has had two major effects on information professionals. First, an understanding of automation systems and networking has become a fundamental need; any information professional must have at least a basic knowledge of the ways in which computers operate and the tasks that can be accomplished by automation. Second, there is a growing need for information professionals who are automation experts. The automation needs of libraries and similar information institutions are inherently different from those of stores, manufacturers, and other businesses. Frequently the bodies of data that need to be manipulated are very large and very complex, and they must be tailored to meet varied and complex information needs. Effectively planning, designing, and implementing an automated information system is a difficult task requiring special skills. The information professionals who undertake such activities may have any number of titles: systems analyst, library automation specialist, and database manager are examples. These professionals are required to have a thorough understanding of the needs of information agencies and the ways in which computer technology can meet those needs.

Administration

We have already described a typical day in the life of a public and academic library director. The work of the administrator in the information professions closely parallels the work of any administrator in the public sector. The central concern for administrators is planning—planning to ensure that the information institution they direct is continually developing its services to meet the needs of the community served. In very large libraries, planning and public relations may take up most of the administrator's time. In smaller institutions, personnel and budgeting also come under the purview of the administrator.

Most administrators have come up through the ranks and thus have firsthand knowledge of the various activities carried out in libraries and are able to interpret that work to others within the system. Those with administrative responsibilities often take on policy-making positions within the state or national library and information associations and work not only to develop services in their own institution but to enhance the quality of information provision in general.

The range of administrative positions in the information professions is great. The director of a corporate information center may have a small, highly trained, computer-oriented staff that works with a specialized subject matter. An example of this type of position would be management of an advertising firm's information center, with a focus on several large client accounts that deal with processed dairy products or soybean derivatives. On the other hand, the director of a large urban library may manage a central facility housing more than a million volumes and dozens of branch locations—an operation employing hundreds of people.

The manager of any information agency, regardless of its size, must be flexible, adaptable, and knowledgeable about the rapidly changing technologies that make for an efficient provision of information and the materials that contain it. The administrator must be well versed in both public and technical service aspects of the institution managed and able to work with many types of people.

SPECIALIZATION BY TYPE OF MATERIAL

Some information professionals' focus is defined by the type of material with which they work. Data librarians who organize large collections of data for analysis must devise special routines for storing, formatting, and retrieving from CD-ROMs. Photography librarians must catalog their collections with special attention to scale and size and develop retrieval systems that permit comparison of variable techniques. Music librarians provide analytic entries to their collections that take into account both composers and performers.

One of the most common of these specialties would be the film or videotape librarian, who selects films and videotapes for purchase, plans programs with other library colleagues as well as with the general public, and encourages good use of the library's collection of films, videotapes, and other nonprint media.

Because most libraries in schools and community colleges have moved rapidly in the development of collections that include great varieties of nonprint media, the librarians who work there probably have their assignments divided in ways other than by assignment of responsibility for nonprint alone. An example of that kind of assignment according to material type can be seen in school districts where a school library media specialist has responsibility for all professional materials to be used by teachers or for the collection of curriculum materials gathered from within the district and from other parts of the country.

Another kind of specialty by type of material is that of the map librarian. Federal libraries, academic libraries, public libraries, and special libraries may all have map librarians on their staffs. Their skills need to include the ability to interpret and organize map collections. Because of the practical problems of handling odd-sized maps and globes, this is a specialization where appropriate background in academic areas related to geography is important.

The same principles hold true for government information librarians who may be responsible not only for United States documents but also for those from such agencies as the United Nations and state and local governments. These documents may be integrated into a library's general collection, or they may be housed separately so that users may find all government documents in one place. Increasingly government information is available on the Internet. The formats of government documents may vary, but this is another instance where the origin of the material determines the specialty to which it is assigned.

Production of Media

Of increasing importance in all types of information centers is production of media. In more sophisticated systems, this includes the use of hypermedia, live and taped television productions, preparation of graphics, and individualized computer-assisted instruction software. Demand for these more sophisticated media requires staff members with special skills in production and design of exhibits and with graphic talent and ability.

Cable television has opened up new responsibilities for the information professional assigned to media production. In many cities the public library has been designated its own cable channel. As this trend continues, media skills will become more important to the library wishing to provide a full range of service to its public.

Like technical services, these production services require that the personnel involved have a sense of the eventual uses of their materials. The personnel with these responsibilities sometimes are associated with a public service or public relations department, or they may be considered an adjunct of technical services or of the general media program.

INFORMATION SCIENCE

Some information science positions are quite different from those filled by librarians. The training of both types of professional, however, is generally through a school of library and information science. The two fields are closely allied.

The American Society for Information Science describes four major categories of positions in the information science field.

Operation of Information System   Abstractor-indexers process the intellectual content of documents for convenient retrieval, usually through on-line terminals operated by bibliographic searchers. These searchers may work full-time at keyboard terminals or may double as information services librarians. As demand for services in this area grows, most larger public libraries and many academic libraries will find it important to employ individuals with these skills. Most special libraries serving business or industry already have access to such services and employ specialists in computerized bibliographic searching.

Database managers analyze, manipulate, and coordinate raw data in numeric format for efficient use by researchers and management. This may mean the systematization of a company's production records or implementation of large data sets of survey data for social research use by the company.

Microform technologists, individuals who use a wide range of sophisticated equipment to miniaturize or reproduce documents of other records, work closely with publishers and computer specialists developing new services that may never be presented in paper format.

Management of Information Systems   Within an organization, information services, records management, information storage and retrieval, and consulting on communication flow all may be coordinated by a single manager to whom many individuals report. The development of even broader services, such as national networks of specialized information, is sometimes overseen by the information systems manager.

Design of Information Systems   Applications or systems programmers write large-scale computer programs to solve information problems in fields such as business, science, or education. Information consultants advise management of marketing strategy or business expansion through information systems. The information needs of decision makers are filled through automated systems designed and implemented by the management information systems specialist.

Research and Teaching   Computational linguists analyze word and language structures to determine how the computer can manipulate text for editing, indexing, classifying, abstracting, searching, or retrieving.

Cyberneticists study the communication and manipulation of information and its use in controlling the behavior of biological, physical, and chemical systems. Teaching in all the areas outlined as information science usually includes basic research on the phenomena of information. Positions in information science are found in libraries, data-processing centers, industry, and government. The growth of the importance of information means that new careers are being generated all the time. Education in library and information science provides the ideal preparation for this burgeoning field.

OPPORTUNITIES FOR INFORMATION
PROFESSIONALS IN OTHER SETTINGS

Just as it is true that not everyone who works in an information institution such as a library is a librarian, it is true that not all librarians work in libraries. Because librarians often have come from other academic fields with advanced academic background, they have opportunities to combine their information skills with that background; that combination may lead them away from positions in libraries. Also, they may develop new specialties that make positions outside library settings available to them.

Archivists   Many librarians and information scientists have taken on the responsibilities for the archives of their educational institutions. As the work of that area has increased and they have developed expertise in archival work—through experience, further education, or a combination of the two—they have chosen to become archivists. The work requires many of the same competencies that librarianship requires. Although such vocational shifts may be made gradually over several years, the result is that a person who began work as a librarian has actually moved into another professional area. The archivist works with acquisition (sometimes requiring active searching for materials among the papers of individuals or in the bulky records of an institution), the organization, and the use of manuscript materials, records (which may include personnel records, ledgers, or promotional materials), and other items (as varied as an executive's desk set or the time capsule placed in the cornerstone of a corporation's new building). The purpose is preservation of the historical record of the association, movement, or corporation. It should be clearly understood that not all archivists are librarians, but that this is a specialization into which many librarians have moved successfully.

Publishing   Another area of specialization is that of editorial work and other positions in the general area of publishing. There are several professional journals that serve librarianship and information science, and their staff members often have had education and experience in those specialties. Although such positions are few, the individuals who hold them often move on to more general editorial responsibilities in book publishing, often related to the library and information fields. The attention to details, the sense of the needs of users of reference materials, and the desire to provide for those needs are typically characteristics that information professionals share with the editors of such reference aids as indexes, abstracting services, and directories. Thus, it is natural that many librarians have become valued members of such staffs. In administrative posts of publishing firms, some former librarians, who usually began their publishing activities by advising publishers about the needs of the library field, have found interesting positions that are also important for the library and information fields.

In quite a different way, librarians with sound knowledge of a particular market for publishers sometimes have been sought for work in promoting materials to libraries. Some general trade publishers, for example, maintain departments of school and library promotion, where the personnel need to know what kinds of announcements, catalogs, and other publicity techniques will be most appealing to the large library market. In many cases they also maintain close communication with some members of the library profession who play important roles in the selection of materials. Sometimes the value of having been a former library colleague may be quite significant, and many of the people in school and library promotion have come from the library field.

The close link between librarians who work with children and the staff members of juvenile departments of trade publishers is based on an interesting history. In the early years of this century, children's librarians became more and more interested in encouraging the publication of good children's books. When separate departments of editorial positions for children's books were established, it was natural that many of those posts would be filled by children's librarians. Although this is still true today, these positions now are being filled by people from a great variety of backgrounds, of which librarianship is only one.

One part of editorial work and writing in which librarians continue to be prominent is that of reviewing. In many libraries, librarians prepare short, readable, evaluative notes on books and other materials. In these they comment briefly on the content, compare the new item with others available, and note its value in terms of its format, price, and availability. These same skills are important for journals that publish large numbers of reviews. Where staff members do the writing, their members may come from the ranks of librarians; when the journal relies on outside reviewers, a large number of them may be librarians who did this as a professional service or for a fee.

Multimedia Librarians   As the scope of the materials resources available to libraries has broadened, some librarians have moved into positions of new responsibility that reflect that expansion. For example, there may be administrative reasons why it is desirable to have one person responsible for all aspects of materials in a community college; therefore, the former director of the library may become the administrator for the entire educational media program, with responsibilities for television production as well as utilization of all other media. From that, a move to an administrative post with responsibility for the operation of the bookstore or for other curricular areas, such as administration of the educational program for library technical assistants, may be made. The determining factors in the expansion of an individual's career in this way are usually competence, interest in a diversity of fields, and willingness to take some risks in achieving goals.

Information Brokers   A comparatively recent development is the possibility of librarians forming agencies or companies of their own to provide information service to industries, writers, or other groups that require work of this kind. A librarian may do this individually, but there are advantages in several working together—they may be able to function as a team when work is at a peak in order to utilize individual skills and knowledge more effectively. Genealogical searching, long a province for freelancers, is one kind of research in which they may engage; but they may also verify citations for writers, gather a number of references for someone who knows in general what he or she wants but does not have the time to find and organize it, and prepare notes for other researchers, based on their actual reading of reference materials.

Information Consulting   Information scientists have the same kinds of freelance possibilities open to them. Their special competencies may include bibliographic searching of on-line information systems, preparing technical reports as editors or writers, or preparing large-scale computer programs for information storage and retrieval. In these specializations, as well as in librarianship, there are also possibilities for people to work as consultants, perhaps advising on major purchases or selections of systems, making recommendations of building projects, conducting initial searches and interviews for major personnel appointments, advising on the development of media collections, or providing, on a fee basis, their expertise in some other area requiring research.

Usually consultants of this kind are those whose competence has been recognized because of the work they have done in their regular full-time positions. The good decisions made by a library administrator during the planning and construction of a new library, for instance, may cause another administrator to invite her or him to serve as consultant in another building program; or the reputation that a bibliographer develops in selecting materials for the library where he or she works may cause another library to seek his or her assistance when considering major purchases in areas with which its own staff may be less familiar.

Because consultants' work is almost always based on extensive experience, and because employment possibilities are difficult to predict in this kind of work, it is a specialty that information professionals often practice when they retire from full-time work. Being able to combine retirement with work that supplements income and provides change of scene and experience is a very appealing prospect to many retirees.

Perhaps another word might be said here about consultants. Library personnel who see a consultant come into a library in the morning, perhaps fresh from the airport and carrying a suitcase, and who see her or him leave at the end of the day, evidently off to a new assignment, may characterize the work as glamorous. They also may be critical when they see the budget item for the consultant's work. They are probably not aware, however, of the extensive study the consultant may do in advance of each visit and the high pressure and tension under which she or he may have to work while on the scene, just as they may not consider the amount of time she or he may need to spend in preparing and presenting a report on her or his findings. Such reports may go to a board of trustees or a general administrator rather than to the library's own administrator, and they are certain to prompt questions the consultant must be prepared to answer. Professional knowledge, personal confidence, common sense, experience, ability to think on one's feet, and willingness to acknowledge errors are major components of consulting work. And, as mentioned, the individuals who work their way into such positions have usually done so after long years in other kinds of responsible supervisory or administrative work.

Professional Association Work   In addition to these self-employed library and information specialists, there are others who work in neither libraries nor information centers but nonetheless need a thorough knowledge of their field. For example, staff positions in the various national library and information associations are most often filled by librarians who may serve as consultants or representatives. They work as association managers with other professional people, travel extensively to conferences, prepare promotional materials for their associations, and handle many other tasks that need to be done when officers of such associations have only limited time for their responsibilities. Since many librarians often have had on-the-job experience with similar responsibilities, they are good choices for such posts.

A growing number of state and regional library and information associations also employ staff persons. Although not all of these are information professionals, they often come from the ranks of library employees because they need to be familiar with the work of their colleagues in the association. Additionally, they may be called upon to represent the views of the information profession in general. Their public relations responsibilities may include lobbying for state or national legislations, making the public aware of the significance of libraries and information centers, and organizing conferences or conventions where educational programs for members, the business of the association, exhibits of professional materials and library equipment, and entertainment all need to be coordinated effectively. These positions, like those in the various national associations of librarians and information scientists, are highly visible and influential; but the demands they make in terms of travel and general workload often mean that the individuals who accept such positions work in them for only a few years. Since there is a need for practitioners in the field to know something of the workings of their associations and for the associations' staff members to be conversant with the field's work and views, this kind of interchange is probably healthy.

Library and Information Science Faculty Members Another specialty within the information professions that is usually arrived at after experience in the field is that of faculty member in a college or university program. Some teach in undergraduate education programs, preparing students to be school library media specialists, supervising them in their fieldwork in school library media centers, and teaching such courses as children's literature and basic cataloging. Other educators may have responsibility for students enrolled in two-year or one-year library technical assistant programs, where their course work may include introductory courses in librarianship. These educators also may be responsible for advising students as they take such courses as business English, typing and filing, or others that are not limited in scope to libraries but are relevant to the work for which they are preparing. These library educators also may have responsibility for supervising their students on field assignments; and they also may need to be concerned with the placement of their students, especially in their first positions.

Educators who are faculty members in graduate programs of education for the information professions may be teaching courses that are somewhat more theoretical than those offered at the undergraduate level and are directed toward a great variety of prospective information careers. In institutions where doctoral programs in library and information science are offered, educators' responsibilities include research, publishing, and close liaison with the field through their work as consultants or teachers in continuing education programs.

The full-time faculty members in any kind of information education programs usually provide most of the instruction; but their work often is strengthened by that of practicing librarians who teach in their areas of expertise, perhaps on a regular part-time basis or for a summer session or workshop. Usually, the full-time faculty members must meet all requirements for faculty appointments at their institutions; doctoral degrees often are a part of this requirement. Research ability, teaching, competence, and experience are other desirable characteristics.

Because librarianship is a profession that requires knowledge of administration, management, and organization of information, and because it may be related to such areas as publishing, historical research, communication, and formal education, the faculty members of library education programs often have come from other areas of specialization. Social scientists, linguists, engineers, publishers, and educational administrators are among those who have served effectively on the faculties of some programs. From this it's apparent that positions in information education are not limited to librarians. Also, since the work of admissions and placement, the editing of school publications, and other varied work may not require the expertise of a faculty member, there may be others, some of them librarians, who work in library education programs in these kinds of positions.

Information science programs in institutions of higher education usually are designed so that faculty members in many different specialties teach in them. Research in information science usually is performed by faculty members in these programs, and, in this fairly new field, they are often key people in determining the nature of the field and its future.

As can be seen from this survey of places of library employment and types of library positions, the diversity of opportunities is extraordinary. Whatever one's interest, special background, or education, there is likely to be a type of library work appropriate.

THE WORK OF SUPPORT STAFF

Although this book primarily addresses the career opportunities for professionally trained information professionals, we need to take note of the variety of personnel necessary to ensure the proper running of a library or information center.

In libraries, as in other places of employment, there is a need for a variety of support personnel. Word processors, maintenance engineers, and security officers are only a few of the kinds of support staff employed. In most instances their duties in a library may not differ very much from what they might be in another work setting. A guard, for example, who patrols a large academic library on a regular basis, checking for fires, vandalism, or someone in trouble, may really be doing the same kind of work that an industrial plant guard might perform. Though these jobs are important to libraries, the people who perform them usually do not consider themselves as being in library careers. There are, however, many support staff who do not hold a master's degree but who do have careers in library and information settings.

Library Technician   An important member of the support staff is the library technician, sometimes designated as library technical assistant (LTA). The library technician usually is a person who has completed two years of academic work, often in a community college, emphasizing the learning of library skills. More information about such training programs appears later, but it may be said here that library technicians are prepared to work in public service areas as well as in technical services. Circulation routines, work on the physical preparation of books (labeling, duplicating cards, assisting with placement of orders), and such individual specialties as assisting with the maintenance and use of audiovisual equipment may be the regular work of library technicians.

Library technicians, like librarians, often are able to utilize in library work the skills that they have acquired elsewhere. The ability to work in graphics may be applied to the preparation of instructional transparencies in a school library media center, the production of signs and exhibits for an entire public library system, or the design of an information center's annual report in a special library.

In recent years many people have attended programs training them for library technical assistance and have received academic credit, associate degrees, and certificates of their completion of such programs. At the same time demand for library technicians has been so great that others have found exactly the kinds of positions they sought without finishing their educational programs. Their on-the-job training has enabled them to become valued members of library teams because of their particular libraries' procedures. Consequently they often have felt no need to return to a campus to complete a training program for library technical assistants. Some libraries have used the designation of library technical assistant for many members of their specialized support staff despite the fact that they may not meet specific LTA educational requirements. Although those trained only on-the-job have competed with academically trained LTAs for jobs, it is possible that, in the future, educational programs for LTAs will prove themselves so superior as a personnel source that libraries will insist on this kind of education as a prerequisite for employment. At present, however, it is more likely that libraries will continue to employ people with a mix of academic backgrounds in technical assistant positions. Because their competencies may be more related to one library than to others, those who have not completed formal training programs may find their mobility from one library to another somewhat limited.

Members of the support staff who have some library experience may serve in such responsible positions as heads of circulation services, supervisors of clerical and technical personnel in some large departments, or supervisors of such support staff as equipment maintenance workers, drivers, and others. These supervisory positions customarily require unusual knowledge about the library, willingness to accept responsibility and to exercise authority, and special supervisory abilities in dealing with people. Such positions tend to be among the best available to members of the support staff, offering many satisfactions.

Library Assistant   Another important member of the library support staff is the library assistant. Library assistants organize library resources and make them available to users. They assist librarians and, in some cases, library technicians.

Library assistants—sometimes referred to as "library media assistants," "library aides," or "circulation assistants"—register patrons so they can borrow materials from the library. They record the borrower's name and address from an application and then issue a library card. Most library assistants enter and update patrons' records using computer databases.

At the circulation desk, assistants lend and collect books, periodicals, videotapes, and other materials. When an item is borrowed, assistants stamp the due date on the material and record the patron's identification from his or her library card. They inspect returned materials for damage, check due dates, and compute fines for overdue material. They review records to compile a list of overdue materials and send out notices. They also answer patrons' questions and refer those they cannot answer to a librarian.

Throughout the library, assistants sort returned books, periodicals, and other items and return them to their designated shelves, files, or storage areas. They locate materials to be loaned, either for a patron or another library. Many card catalogs are computerized, so library assistants must be familiar with the computer system. If any materials have been damaged, these workers try to repair them. For example, they use tape or paste to repair torn pages or book covers and other specialized processes to repair more valuable materials.

Some library assistants specialize in helping patrons who have vision problems. Sometimes referred to as "library clerks," "talking-books clerks," or "Braille-and-talking-books clerks," they review the borrower's list of desired reading material. They locate those materials or closely related substitutes from the library collection of large type or Braille volumes, tape cassettes, and open-reel talking books. They complete the paperwork and give or mail them to the borrower.

Bookmobile Driver   To extend library services to more patrons, many libraries operate bookmobiles. Bookmobile drivers take trucks stocked with books to designated sites on a regular schedule. Bookmobiles serve community organizations, such as shopping centers, apartment complexes, schools, and nursing homes. They also may be used to extend library service to patrons living in remote areas. Depending on local conditions, drivers may operate a bookmobile alone or may be accompanied by a library technician.

When working alone, the drivers perform many of the same functions as a library assistant in a main or branch library. They answer patrons' questions, receive and check out books, collect fines, maintain the book collection, shelve materials, and occasionally operate audiovisual equipment to show slides or films. They participate and may assist in planning programs sponsored by the library, such as reader advisory programs, used book sales, or outreach programs. Bookmobile drivers keep track of their mileage, the materials lent out, and the amount of fines collected. In some areas, they are responsible for maintenance of the vehicle and any photocopiers or other equipment in it. They record statistics on circulation and the number of people visiting the bookmobile. Drivers also may record requests for special items from the main library and arrange for the materials to be mailed or delivered to a patron during the next scheduled visit. Many bookmobiles are equipped with personal computers and CD-ROM systems linked to the main library system; this allows bookmobile drivers to reserve or locate books immediately. Some bookmobiles now offer Internet access to users.

Because bookmobile drivers may be the only link some people have to the library, much of their work is helping the public. They may assist handicapped or elderly patrons to the bookmobile, or shovel snow to ensure their safety. They may enter hospitals or nursing homes to deliver books to patrons who are bedridden. The schedules of bookmobile drivers depend on the size of the area being served. Some of these workers go out on their routes every day, while others go only on certain days. On these other days, they work at the library. Some also work evenings and weekends to give patrons as much access to the library as possible.

Because such factors as personality, interest, and general competence in library-related skills are important in many support positions, these positions frequently are filled by workers who have no intention of remaining in them for any length of time but who value them either for the relevant experience or for the kind of employment opportunity they present at the time. Members of students' families, for example, often need employment for the period of the student's enrollment at a college or university, just as the students themselves often need part-time employment. Some positions may regularly be designated for these individuals as a part of the academic institution's internal economy. Another category of people who may seek support positions on a short-term basis are those who are planning to enroll in library and information science education programs and who want some kind of library experience. This, of course, means that there is considerable turnover of personnel and is one reason why the position of supervisor of the support staff is an especially challenging one; staff morale and programs of in-service education become especially important in these circumstances.

The long hours that libraries usually are open require competent staff during evenings and on weekends, traditionally the times when many people want to be free. Because of this, work for night service supervisors, security personnel, pages, and circulation personnel may be available. These positions also may appeal to students or others with daytime responsibilities. The work of reshelving materials or preparing materials to be delivered to other library agencies may be done more efficiently at times when there are fewer users in the library, so these evening hours may be peak activity times for the staff.

Although the people who work at the charging desks of libraries are from the clerical or technical assistance ranks, they are extremely important in establishing the climate and purpose of the library. Informal comments by these staff members about some of the library's services may stimulate users to make the most of what else is available to them. The rapport established at the circulation desk is the beginning of good interaction between the user and the library.

More service is provided to the public at a circulation desk or in a circulation department than may be visible to someone simply watching people returning or borrowing library materials. When someone has requested a specific book by title, or even by subject, for example, the circulation files may be checked to determine when it is due and who has borrowed it. Some libraries may provide the service of requesting its return; others may promise to reserve it when it is returned. Either of these is an important service to the reader; both require accurate records of information and careful attention to details of book circulation.

THE INFORMATION SOCIETY

As the world becomes more reliant on quickly relayed information for decision making, the need for individuals skilled in managing information will increase. From traditional professional positions in libraries to evolving positions in information centers, the opportunities for skilled personnel seem limitless. Careers range from supportive to managerial or professional, and different levels of education prepare individuals to enter this work. In the next chapter the type of education required for employment in the information society is outlined.

CHAPTER 3

EDUCATION FOR THE
INFORMATION PROFESSIONS

Librarians and information scientists come from a variety of educational backgrounds. Sometimes their early schooling has been designed by them as background for their future careers; often it may lead them to these careers because their later experience suggests a change of direction. Professional and technical careers in librarianship and information science require carefully planned educational programs.

Preparation for clerical positions in librarianship is not different in any significant way from preparation for other kinds of clerical positions. High school graduation or equivalent background, knowledge of office skills and routines, and interest in learning on the job are important for the person seeking a position of this kind.

Administrators and supervisors who may work in the business offices of libraries, are personnel officers, or fill such posts as those of public relations specialists in libraries usually have followed educational programs that prepare them for those special fields. In some cases they have combined this preparation with information education or have made special efforts during their work experience to develop expertise about libraries and information centers.

HIGH SCHOOL

Very few of the people who later become librarians and information scientists make their career decisions before they enter college; however, many find that decisions they make about which subjects to take in high school do become important later. Usually their high school programs are designed to prepare them for college. In most states, the requirements for academic units in the social sciences, literature, sciences, and mathematics are sufficient for the individual who later enters a career in library and information science. Study of one or more foreign languages may be valuable for people selecting careers in these fields. For practical reasons courses, such as typing, though not usually part of the precollegiate program, may prove valuable both for the future college student preparing papers and for the future professional in information science who will work with computers on-line.

Extracurricular activities may be good indicators of future interests and also may provide experience useful in later years. Work as a computer tutor, library assistant, or media aide during high school will prepare you for a future career; however, you should be aware of the possibility that, if such work stresses only the routine aspects of library work, it could serve to convince you that librarianship is too boring for you. That is a false impression, however, because you may find that the responsibilities in the more creative professional library offer the kind of challenge that is missing in the work of shelving books, writing overdue slips, delivering projectors to classrooms on schedule, or similar tasks.

What may be important in your work as a student assistant in a computer center library is experience with responsibility and recognition of the need for behind-the-scenes, unglamorous work. You will have an opportunity to learn the importance of schedules on public service desks and the need for tact in dealing with the library's users. These kinds of information and experience are worth acquiring, but they can be acquired in other experiences as well: staffing concession stands at athletic games, working on the school newspaper, or accepting leadership roles in student government.

High school years also may be the time when young people make serious efforts to explore various careers. Many young people who have no interest at all in information work become intrigued when they have an opportunity even to read about or, better yet, to visit and observe other kinds of libraries or information centers. Counselors can be important in stimulating interest and suggesting visits and interviews, as well as reading materials, which may be helpful.

If this kind of counseling is not available but you sense that some kind of information-related work may be what you have in mind, you may start by interviewing librarians you know, asking them about their own backgrounds and the satisfactions they have found in the field, as well as what suggestions they might have to offer. You can integrate these recommendations best if you consider them in terms of how relevant they are to your own career and life goals. For example, if the school librarian tells you that it was only after twenty years of teaching that he or she decided to enter librarianship and that everyone should start with long teaching experience, you may wish to weigh that advice against your own eagerness to get started in a profession in which you want to spend most of your working years. Since there will be differences of opinion, the final decision will have to be yours, with the advice of others only contributing to your pool of information.

CHOOSING A COLLEGE

The choice of a college can be critical in regard to your later career. Certainly if you intend to study information issues during your college years, you should plan to enter a college where this is offered regularly as part of a planned program. Often this will mean courses that are part of the education or teacher-training program. You should find out whether the college is accredited by a regional accrediting agency and whether the program of teacher education is accredited by the national agency that evaluates such curricula. Direct inquiries at the time of application can usually provide this information.

Many universities are now developing undergraduate programs in information studies. At universities that offer graduate work in library and information science, it often is possible to enroll in some of these courses while you are still an undergraduate.

The choice of a college is important for anyone who plans to study librarianship or information science at the graduate level. You should be concerned with the quality of the college and find out whether it is accredited by the appropriate regional accrediting agency.

You should make sure that the school offers the blend of structure and flexibility you want from your college courses. You should find out whether such features as study abroad are available, since this can be a good way to improve your language competence. You should make certain, as early as possible and preferably before enrolling, that the program you want to follow is really feasible and that the major you have in mind can be changed without penalties of lost time—in short, that the college can provide what you believe you want at this time and what you may later realize you want and need before graduation. The success of the college's graduates in being admitted to the graduate programs of their choice is not easily measured, but you should inquire about it, both formally and informally, if you have an opportunity to talk with students and graduates from the college.

With all these considerations, in selecting a college you need to keep in mind that the college experience should be satisfying in itself, providing you with knowledge, experience, friends, memories, and opportunity in rich supply. Since you, your family, and the college will, in a sense, be investing in your future, your choice of a college is crucial for more reasons than its effect on your possible opportunities in a career.

The choice of a program for education as a library technical assistant usually is more restricted and often may be delayed for some years after high school graduation. Since most of these programs are in two-year community colleges, students who enroll in them usually come from the surrounding area. Those who are interested may wish to verify how frequently the various courses are offered, how many instructors there are for the courses, and what measures of success there are for the students who have completed the programs in terms of placement opportunities, advancement on the job, and other important factors.

Background for Graduate Education in the Information Professions

There is scarcely a subject area that does not relate to one of the information fields. A broad undergraduate preparation in the liberal arts is the best preparation for success in the information professions. Certain types of library and information centers such as agricultural libraries or toxicology research institutes may require a specific undergraduate concentration, but in general any undergraduate preparation can be used in an information center.

Computer literacy is necessary if you plan to enter the information professions. More and more library and information retrieval functions continue to become computer-based, and all information professionals will be required to understand computer applications. Other undergraduate courses that might be useful include foreign languages, statistics, communications, business management, and research.

SELECTING A LIBRARY
AND INFORMATION SCIENCE PROGRAM

The college years are the time when students need to carefully consider the exact requirements of the library and information science education programs that they wish to enter at the graduate level. Preparation of applications, gathering of letters of reference, planning for financial arrangements for study, taking required tests, and arranging for interviews or visits to the campus all usually take more time than students think they will. For the student who intends to start graduate school immediately or within a few months after college graduation, these procedures probably should be started early in the senior year.

Before applying to schools, of course, you will want to select the three or four that most appeal to you. A letter or telephone call requesting their catalog and application form should be answered promptly. More specific questions may be directed to the schools when you go for an interview or when you write or call the next time. The catalog should answer the most important questions about the school's academic program:

- What are requirements for admission?
- What is the school's job placement record?
- Is financial aid available?
- What are the prospects for part-time employment?
- Who are the faculty?
- How large is the student body?

The answers to these questions may prompt others about housing near the school, access to research libraries, and availability of other programs of financial assistance.

There are numerous scholarships and fellowships for graduate study in librarianship and information science, often announced in the various professional journals and compiled by such organizations as the American Library Association. In addition service clubs, alumni groups, small foundations, church groups, or others may offer financial assistance for which the prospective student may qualify. There is usually much competition for the major scholarship and fellowship programs; while that should not deter you from trying to get such assistance, you should also apply for smaller grants for which fewer people may apply or be eligible. Of course the stipulations of individual scholarship programs should be kept in mind. There is no point in applying for scholarships for which you are clearly ineligible or accepting one when you do not intend to live up to its stipulations, such as requiring the recipient to work in a public library in a given state for a set period of time after graduation from a program of library and information science.

The answers you get to your first questions may help you decide which library and information science program you wish to attend, but it is still wise to apply to more than one for many reasons. You may not be accepted by your first choice; you can then move on to your second or even third choice with less effort if you have made several applications at the start of your search for a school.

It is desirable to choose a school where the master's degree program in library and information science is accredited by the American Library Association (ALA). The ALA accredits programs in both the United States and Canada. The standards for accreditation published by the association cover such areas as faculty, students, physical facility, administration, governance, and curriculum. Some of these may seem to affect students only in an indirect way, but the extent to which a school is autonomous within the university or college may be important if decisions about budget need to be made or if decisions about who shall be admitted are made without consideration of their possible contributions to the field of library and information science. Accreditation in itself does not mean that one program is superior to another that has not sought accreditation or has not achieved it for other reasons, but it does mean that the program has been studied and assessed carefully and that an outside agency has considered the program a good one. Graduation from an accredited program is important when one is seeking employment and might be considered an absolute requirement by many employers.

Many people may graduate from college and decide to take some time off from study and classwork before continuing their education. This is quite common among those entering the information professions. A number of second-career people or reentry individuals have entered library and information careers and used their previous education and experience fruitfully.

The scope of information careers ranges from support staff to public or technical service to administration and teaching. Each level of employment requires a different category of educational preparation.

LIBRARY AND INFORMATION CENTER
TECHNICAL ASSISTANT PROGRAMS

Community college programs are the most common for focused training of library and information center technical assistants. Today the positions for which students in these programs are being prepared are not always clearly defined, but the term library technical assistant (LTA) has become the most common one to describe people who have completed the course work. Some libraries and information centers have included in their personnel structures positions designed for these individuals to fill. More often the library and information center technical assistants have created positions for themselves that utilize their skills effectively.

And what are those skills? It is generally recognized that some postsecondary education of a general nature (English, word processing, computer programming, or accounting, perhaps) is needed for library and information center technical assistants. But their area of concentration still probably includes courses introducing them to the information professions in general, so that they are aware of the many types of libraries, their patterns of services and purposes, and general trends. Circulation work and technical services are two areas where LTAs are more likely to be assigned; courses that teach routines of filing, record-keeping, and general bibliographic control and electronic communications are a part of the curricula. Many programs include specific courses in the production of graphics, the production and utilization of other media, and an introduction to some information seeking skills. Fieldwork or practice work in neighboring libraries is often a part of the student's academic program also. This feature can be a definite asset if good performance leads to placement in the system of the library where the student has performed fieldwork.

Most programs of education for LTAs are in two-year community colleges, but they may be one- or two-year programs. The component of the program dealing with the work of library and information center technical assistants may be designed to be the second year, following a more general first year of study. The programs often are closely related to the learning resources center in the community the college services. The practical emphasis of these programs, however, is such that their graduates often have much to offer in the way of skills, and they usually find placement no problem.

The people most likely to be happy in the careers for which LTA education will prepare them are those who want to work in libraries or media centers, using their special skills and possibly becoming the supervisor of others who are performing technical work in those libraries. Some further specialization, perhaps in book repair, development of more skills related to electronic resources, or work on computer network systems may be possible on the job, but advancement to professional positions is indeed unlikely in most library and information center settings without further education.

Employers typically require applicants to have at least a high school diploma or its equivalent, though many employers might prefer to hire assistants with a higher level of education. Regardless of formal qualifications, most employers prefer workers who are computer literate. Knowledge of word processing and spreadsheet software is especially valuable, as are experience working in an office and good interpersonal skills.

Once hired, records processing clerks usually receive on-the-job training. Under the guidance of a supervisor or other senior worker, new employees learn company procedures and database maintenance skills. Some formal classroom training also may be necessary, such as training in specific computer software.

COLLEGE COURSES IN LIBRARY AND INFORMATION SCIENCE

Education for information careers that is begun as part of undergraduate education is less common today than it was thirty or forty years ago. The demand for greater specialization, a broad liberal arts or science background, and the availability of educational programs at the graduate level in library and information science have caused many colleges that offered minors or majors in librarianship to drop their courses, or, in some instances, to make drastic revisions resulting in the courses becoming graduate-level programs.

Recently, however, a number of graduate programs in library and information science have reassessed the role of undergraduate study. Information resources management programs have been instituted that are intended to prepare individuals to combine another undergraduate major with a major in information studies. Since this movement is relatively new, prospective students who wish to major in the information sciences at the undergraduate level should contact an accredited program of library and information science listed in Appendix B for further information.

School Library Media Specialization
at the Undergraduate Level

The need for school library media specialists and the fact that many of their educational programs are as closely associated with schools or departments of education as they are with schools of library and information science mean that many of these media programs have been designed for students who wish to enter the school library media field. They may be working toward a major in library science or in education, with a minor in the other of the two fields mentioned.

Emphasis   The media center courses in programs of this kind usually stress school library media center administration rather than general library management. Materials that are studied and evaluated in greatest detail are usually those designed for the clientele of school library media centers. Because of the emphasis that school library media centers usually place on instructional technology, these may be studied in greater detail than they would be in graduate programs of library and information science. Because school library media collections are relatively small, the organization of materials may be handled through a central district processing center or through specialized computer programs.

Depending on the rapport between the school library media education program and the program of teacher education at the same institution, there may be considerable emphasis on the teaching aspects of the library or media center. Instruction in how to teach library or study skills may be part of the curriculum; regardless of whether students also are enrolled in the education courses, they are likely to be encouraged or required to take one or more courses introducing them to the general field of elementary or secondary education. Since it is important for school library media specialists to know the milieu of the whole school and to have good general knowledge of the curriculum, these courses may be quite valuable for them.

Certification   Certification is almost universally required in school teaching positions, including library media positions. For that reason most undergraduate programs that prepare librarians for school work are carefully designated so that those completing the program will qualify for certification at least in the state where the institution is located. Two trends are increasing the value of that certification. One is the increase in reciprocity among states. This means that a person who earns a certificate valid in one state may automatically be granted a certificate in another state, even though there may be slight variations in the specific requirements of the two states. The other is the trend toward competency-based education, especially strong in programs of teacher education. This means that the acquisition of a specific group of competencies is recognized as necessary, and if individuals can demonstrate their possession of those competencies, they have met the requirements. In programs like this, the accumulation of academic credit is valueless unless the individual has acquired the competencies judged necessary for the work.

School library media education programs at the undergraduate level customarily have practice or fieldwork in a school library media center as a requirement. This may be taken in conjunction with practice teaching; both may be required at different times, or the library media fieldwork may be sufficient. Because school library media specialists are likely to be employed, at least in their first jobs, in settings where they must work independently and with limited or no access to a supervisor with background in librarianship, it is especially important for them to have the experience of working with a certified media specialist.

There was a time when school library media specialists came exclusively from the ranks of experienced classroom teachers. As recognition of the special background and work of librarians has increased, there have been increasing numbers who entered the field directly. It is still customary for them to have certification as teachers and to have demonstrated, at least through practice teaching, their ability to teach. For that reason, a typical program of courses for a college student intending to become a school library media specialist includes such general courses as English, history, or science, along with professional education courses such as teaching of reading, history of American or western education, and teaching of social studies, curriculum, and educational psychology. The component of library and media science education typically may include children's literature, school media library administration, selection of media, cataloging and classification, reference, and instructional technology.

Computer Literacy   Many state certifying agencies include computer literacy as a requirement for school library media positions. This is for two reasons: (1) Computer laboratories often are located in or adjacent to school library media centers. Since these are a schoolwide resource, they are viewed by school administrators as analogous to the media center in their centrality to the educational enterprise; and (2) Many computer software programs enable school library media librarians to automate their own circulation, acquisitions, and cataloging operations.

As the typical program suggests, this curriculum can be a demanding one, especially since it may include one or more assignments for practice or fieldwork in schools. And the graduate of such a program may be disappointed to discover that some top jobs in the field of school media librarianship, such as district supervisors, may be reserved for those who have completed advanced degrees in library and information science. In fact, most school systems place so much emphasis on the need for continuing education that they encourage librarians to take courses by paying higher salaries to those with advanced degrees or by reimbursing students wholly or partially for their tuition expenses. Many school media specialists who leave their colleges thinking they will take a rest from education find that before long they are taking more courses, either on a part-time basis or during summer school.

Graduates of undergraduate library education programs may decide to pursue other areas of interest in their advanced academic work. Because of the heavy emphasis on professional education courses during their college years, this may be a wise decision. One possibility may be to enter a master's degree program in library and information science with the intention of changing to another specialization within the field. In that case a broad range of courses may be taken, for example, relating to special libraries and their media or to the particular problems of public libraries, as former school media librarians prepare for another phase in their career.

Undergraduate programs of this kind are probably best for people who wish to be able to begin work immediately after college and who are sure that school media librarianship appeals to them. They should recognize that shifts in career goals later may present problems, but that there are many satisfactions in the career for which they are currently preparing. People interested in school library media center work should recognize that many states are moving toward certification requiring a master's degree, so contact should be made with the department of education in the states where you are interested in working to determine the latest qualifications needed.

Library and Information Center Associate Positions

Many libraries have positions designated for library associates, individuals who have completed four years of college, but who may have little or no academic preparation in library or information science. Although positions of this kind may not be satisfying enough for a life's career, they may be attractive to people intending to prepare themselves for librarianship or another career by further study, or those who wish to work in libraries for a few years. Typical of the positions and responsibilities assigned to library associates may be assistance in some of the library's technical services, such as on-line searching for cataloging information; outreach work in public libraries, often with special emphasis on work with children; providing telephone reference service; and assisting with promotional activities of the library, such as editing a newsletter or designing exhibits and graphic materials.

It is rare to find college curricula designed to prepare library associates for their work. Almost any academic background can be helpful to the library associate, from art to zoology. The reliance that libraries have placed on library associates has caused some people to discuss the possibility of more precisely designed academic programs in this area. Included in these programs are undergraduate courses that would be good introductions to satisfying careers in librarianship. If these develop to any extent in the next few years, they may be useful and available for would-be library associates. In the meantime the position of library associate is one that may be sought and filled by college graduates who enjoy work in a library and who want to work where they can use the education, interests, and special skills or knowledge they have acquired.

GRADUATE STUDY FOR THE
INFORMATION PROFESSIONS

Preparation for the information professions at the professional level almost always requires the minimum of a master's degree. The degree may have many names—master of science, master of arts, master of information science, master of library and information science, master of library and information studies—but it denotes the completion of a planned program of study beyond the bachelor's degree, with emphasis on learning not only the skills needed for the information professions but also the philosophy of the professions.

Nearly all librarians attain the master's degree from institutions that provide a major course of study in library and information science. Other aspects of information careers may substitute a master's degree in management information systems through a business administration program or a master's degree in computer science, but today most of these allied fields' subject matter is covered in programs leading to the master's degree in library and information science.

A number of library and information science programs offer joint degrees with departments of computer science, business administration, history (for archival work), law, or other disciplines. These specialties are outlined in the catalogs and bulletins of the programs that offer them.

Master's Degree Courses

The master's degree in library and information science typically offers opportunity for both pursuit of general interests and some degree of specialization that parallels opportunities for professional work. Most students begin with required courses that may include an introduction to information in modern society, basic organizational skills (both manual and computerized), and management concepts. Specialization then occurs through close work with a graduate advisor in such areas as on-line information retrieval, academic librarianship, records management, public librarianship, systems analysis, youth services, indexing and abstracting, school library media, computer applications, health sciences information, or database management.

The course of study is generally from one to two years, depending upon the program. Variations by university can only be identified through writing for catalogs and application information directly to the accredited master's degree programs listed in Appendix B.

The Admissions Process Admission requirements for graduate programs have been mentioned. A written application, perhaps an interview, evidence of foreign language skills, scores on a national examination such as the Graduate Record Examination (GRE) or on one designed by the individual school or university, and letters of reference from people who know the applicant are typical among these requirements.

Requirements for admission usually are clearly detailed in the school's catalog. You should read this and other material from the school carefully, making sure that you understand what is expected of you and what you may expect from the school. Usually, the full range of courses may be listed in the catalog; but some may be limited to students in the doctoral program, if there is one, or some may be offered only occasionally. If you wish to register for some specific courses, you should indicate that in your correspondence or when you visit the school and verify whether those courses will be offered while you are a student. Slight or major changes in the program may occur while you are enrolled, and you should inquire in advance whether a change of requirements will affect you and, if so, in what ways.

There are typically several steps in the process of admission, and it is advisable to check with the school's admissions officer if you do not hear from the school within a reasonable time. A letter of reference may be missing, for instance, and it may be possible to get another one to replace it. The applicant is responsible for checking to be sure that the application is complete.

Courses of Study   One way in which library and information science education programs vary considerably is in the extent to which students are encouraged or permitted to register for courses in other parts of the college or university. In some programs a minor in another field is required; but in most a student probably will take all or nearly all of the courses in the library and information science program. Joint programs with other schools or departments also are available in some universities. Among these are ones that prepare for law librarianship by offering a program of law courses and library and information science courses and similar ones in business administration, education, computer science, and such area studies as Latin America, the Far East, or Southeast Asia. Especially in joint programs of this kind, students are usually at an advantage if they declare their interest in such programs at the time they apply and if they work closely with an adviser in choosing courses so that they fill all necessary requirements as expeditiously as they can.

As in other graduate programs, those in library schools are designed for adults; therefore, emphasis on the importance of an adviser may seem strange. But there is value to your becoming acquainted with at least one faculty member, preferably one who shares many of the same professional interests and, ideally, one with whom you are personally compatible. The adviser who is aware of your interests and intentions, for example, may represent those interests to the faculty when schedule changes are being considered, if those changes should be to your disadvantage. Also, in a large school, you may benefit from some feeling of a tie with at least one member of the faculty, but you may find that you will have to take much of the initiative in maintaining communication with a busy faculty member. Usually you register with your adviser for each term, and one more conversation or brief visit each term may be sufficient.

Graduation Requirements   Requirements for graduation from the master's degree program also should be reviewed. The total number of courses, the core or required courses, the grade average that must be maintained, the preparation of a thesis or research project, and the passing of a comprehensive examination all are considerations among these requirements. The student who wants to design a highly individualized study program would do well to avoid a school where most of the courses are specified as required, with little choice of electives.

Even if the school's requirements are fairly flexible, you must exercise judgment in designing a program for yourself. It is tempting to select a great variety of courses on the theory that you will then be ready for any kind of information work; but the employer who looks at an array of courses taken by a graduate—one course in each of three types of library administration or courses that range from data structures to government documents with no set evidence of purpose or goal—is simply puzzled about the individual's interest and goals rather than impressed by a broad spectrum of skills. Management, bibliographic organization, library materials, and issues for the information society are usually represented in core or basic courses. One value of taking at least one course in each of these areas fairly early in the program is that it may help you decide what you will choose next. Systems analysis, for example, will probably have a prerequisite of introductory computer programming. If you discover you enjoy that kind of study, you may miss the opportunity of studying further if you have postponed taking introductory programming until late in your graduate program. Many choices probably will be available, even in a fairly structured program.

In the earlier section "Selecting a Library and Information Science Program," comments were made about the value of selecting programs accredited by the American Library Association (ALA). During graduate study it may be worthwhile to review the reasons for selecting the program you are in. You should explore ways to benefit from that selection in terms of placement, communications with others in the field who know the school, and the value of keeping in touch with the school after completion of the academic program.

In addition to the courses you take, you often have access to other information and experience through a school's program of colloquium talks; attendance at local, state, or national conferences of library and information associations; and field trips to libraries and information centers. The content of programs may open up new areas of interest or illuminate problems that you have discovered before. But even if that is not the case, the experience of meeting people already in the field and of sitting in on their discussions of their interests and activities can be a valuable part of your professionalization process.

EDUCATION BEYOND THE MASTER'S DEGREE

There are many reasons why you may wish to continue your professional education beyond the master's degree. You may wish to change from one specialization within the field to another. You may need to continue to take courses to receive salary increases or other benefits. You may want to conduct research you think the field needs. You may simply want the intellectual challenge.

It is always worthwhile to ask whether further formal study is really the best means of attaining what you want and whether your goals are realistic. A rigorous program of reading, observing the work of others, and attending conferences or in-service meetings prepares you to enter a new specialization within the field. This type of program may be much more economical in time and energy than enrollment in formal courses.

Another reason for study beyond the master's degree for librarians and information scientists is that they may wish to develop expertise in other academic areas. Just as many people enter the information professions after having acquired advanced degrees elsewhere, information professionals often seek further study in other areas. Sometimes they do this in order to improve their proficiency as librarians—for example, an art librarian works toward a degree in art history, or another librarian who has begun work in personnel decides to become more expert in that field. Occasionally the further study may be simply for pleasure or personal satisfaction, or it may be undertaken by someone who wishes to change to another career.

In the fields of librarianship and information science, there are many programs for post–master's degree study. They differ in purpose and content. Study for a certificate of advanced study, a doctoral degree, and for general continuing education may be appropriate at different points in people's careers. Decisions about pursuing these programs need to be made at different times and with good information about their relative values, scope, and purpose.

Certificates of Advanced Study

In recent years, as interest in continuing professional education has increased, many individuals also have shown interest in working toward some specific goals. Programs of study that awarded certificates indicating that the individual had completed the program were introduced in many schools of library and information science. These are sometimes called "specialist's certificates," "certificates of advanced study," or "sixth-year certificates," the last term indicating that they are awarded for completion of a sixth year of study beyond high school. Customary requirements for these programs are the completion of a group of courses, usually selected in advance from those available in the school of library and information science or elsewhere in the university. A research paper may be required, but research is not a major component of this program. Usually the certificate can be attained in one academic year of full-time study or by part-time study over a longer period of time.

It should be noted that certificate programs are not the same as degree programs. Those who question the awarding of a certificate should keep in mind that it provides recognition for the completion of a set program, not simply for the acquisition of a number of academic credits. The program may be especially good for those who are considering enrolling in a doctoral program but are not sure that their interest and competence are great enough to overcome the obstacles of returning to academic study after working some years. However, the entire thrust of these programs is usually quite different from those of doctoral programs. As noted, certificate programs usually are designed for practitioners in the information field, are short-range in time, and consist chiefly of course work, with success in the courses determining whether one will receive the certificate.

Doctoral Programs

Almost every one of the last three characteristics delineated for certificate programs is the opposite for doctoral study. Doctoral programs are typically more structured, with a series of examinations and set requirements designed by the school offering them. Doctoral programs at one time were designed chiefly for those who wished to devote their careers to teaching and research, but the demand for more skills in the field of administration—especially in the libraries and information centers of research, academic, and school libraries—has led to the development of doctoral programs in which research plays a less significant role. The Ph.D., or Doctor of Philosophy degree, usually indicates research emphasis, while the D.L.S., or Doctor of Library Science degree, usually is classed as a professional degree rather than a research degree. These distinctions are not clear-cut. Some institutions offer one degree but have requirements that make that degree like one with another title elsewhere. The newest doctoral degree in librarianship is that of the Doctor of Arts. It is usually carefully specified as being for practitioners only, with no research component.

Admission to a doctoral program customarily is achieved in a series of steps. The applicant must meet requirements for admission to the school itself, usually identical to those for the master's degree. Because the program's emphasis is likely to be on research, it may be important for the prospective student to have some idea of the desired area of research and a knowledge of the faculty members and other facilities needed for conducting that research.

The courses taken by a doctoral student may, in some instances, be the same as those taken in master's degree programs, especially if some years have elapsed since the doctoral student received the master's degree. Some schools, incidentally, require that students entering the doctoral program must have been working a certain number of years. In any case it is the examinations and research that are important for success in the doctoral program, rather than success in course work. Proof of proficiency in one or more foreign languages also may be required at this stage of a student's program.

The identification of a topic for doctoral research is customarily based on extensive reading, sometimes on preliminary research or feasibility study, and on the interests and abilities of the potential researcher. Usually the student must develop a proposal, stating what he or she intends to do in the research and presenting evidence of the value of the research. A faculty committee probably will review and evaluate the work at that time, perhaps by conducting an oral examination to determine the value of the topic and the student's ability to conduct the research. From that point on in a doctoral program, the student may work almost entirely independently, collecting data for the study, analyzing the data, perhaps traveling to interview individuals who have needed information or insights, and finally writing a dissertation based on the findings. This work also must be defended to some faculty group, usually orally. A faculty committee may be designated as responsible for the doctoral program, deciding on admissions and designing the general examinations. That committee may in turn designate a committee, consisting of the student's adviser and two or three other members, to serve as the student's committee. The defense of the dissertation may be made before the entire faculty, the student's committee, or the doctoral committee. Some recent variations have students presenting this defense before their peers—fellow students or other interested people in the university community—as well. This defense is usually the final step in getting a doctoral degree.

Some schools announce that three years is the customary length of time for students seeking doctoral degrees, but longer periods are not uncommon. The usual difficulty comes in selecting a topic and organizing the findings and data of research. It is at these times that many doctoral candidates withdraw, either formally or informally, from the program. This can be traumatic, not only for the individual but for her or his family, adviser, friends, and colleagues. For this reason it is important that anyone considering a doctoral program should carefully assess the resources—intellectual, physical, and financial—required for the prolonged effort that may be needed.

The kinds of research conducted in the library and information fields at the doctoral level are quite varied. A selection of titles of dissertations gives an idea of the range of topics and methods:

- "A Role Transformed? Technology's Challenge for Job Responsibilities of the Reference Librarian"
- "A Qualitative Study of How Librarians at a Public Research University Envision Their Work and Work Lives"
- "The Role of the High School Library Media Program in Three Nationally Recognized South Carolina Blue Ribbon Secondary Schools"
- "The Changing Print Resource Base of Academic Libraries in the United States: A Comparison of Collection Patterns in Seventy-two ARL Academic Libraries of Nonserial Imprints for the Years 1995 and 2000"

Research is a main link between those who work in the information professions and those engaged in library and information science education. Many investigations of feasibility of innovation techniques have come from research centers in educational programs. The experience of identifying a problem, solving or attempting to solve it, and reporting on the process is often valuable for someone who later becomes a practitioner but must deal with problems in the same way. The objective view of the experienced researcher is important when task forces or other action groups are planning new or revised library programs.

Continuing Education

Information science and librarianship have numerous programs in continuing education, in addition to the more formally constructed programs for doctoral study or certificates of advanced study. The introduction of new techniques, such as computer-assisted reference service, or the continued development of special skills, such as storytelling, are typical purposes of continuing education. Some programs are repeated regularly, as is the case with several university-sponsored programs in library administration and management. Universities, professional and educational associations, and government agencies are the most frequent sponsors of continuing education programs.

Institute, seminar, conference, workshop—these are only four of the designations used for the variety of programs available, and they are often used with no clear distinction among them.

Less readily identified as continuing education programs are the many offerings of library systems, corporations, or educational institutions in which librarians and information specialists are employed. These may include orientation programs for new employees, regularly scheduled meetings for selection of media, programs on new techniques or services, or much more general activities, such as lectures or media presentations introducing personnel to the community or to cultural events. Provision of these programs is one indication of an employer's commitment to continuing education; prospective employees may wish to inquire about such opportunities, as well as about the extent to which the institution may support attendance at other continuing education events.

Somewhat different from the continuing education programs are the conferences sponsored by the associations representing the library and information science professions. Most of these groups sponsor annual conferences at which exhibits of equipment and media, formal meetings, less formal workshops, the business and committee work of the association, social events, placement interviews, and much professional conversation and communication are major events.

The plan for continuing education that is probably best for you is the one that supplies an opportunity to increase your skills or expertise on your present job, offers some satisfaction in the accomplishment of an educational program, and possibly prepares you for another position or a different specialization.

There are many opportunities from which to choose, although your own finances or those of your employer may be major limitations. Within that framework, however, it is possible for you to construct a pattern for yourself that will not only make you more proficient, but also may offer you satisfactions you have not found in your work and lead you to other opportunities where your abilities may be better utilized and developed.

CHAPTER 4

PLACEMENT OF INFORMATION PROFESSIONALS

A major difference between the placement patterns and practices for library and information personnel in positions other than professional ones and those in professional positions is that, in the former instance, the prospective employer and employee are probably concerned only with positions in the locality, while professional positions are more likely to be announced in national publications and recruits sought from a broader geographic area. Because of this, personnel placement in clerical and technical positions is much like placement in other fields. Classified advertisements in newspapers may offer opportunities, or a telephone call to a school system or public library may reveal openings for positions there. Employers also may be interested in suggestions of present employees, so word-of-mouth recommendations may be sought by the person who wants to work in an institution where a friend has found a satisfactory position.

Professional placement, usually handled quite differently, is much more complicated.

INITIAL PLACEMENT

Most people see the first professional position after graduation as significant because it provides them with experience that may be of value later. Additionally it gives them an opportunity to test themselves and their previous education as they learn more about the profession they are entering. Finding and getting this kind of position are worth the energy and thought that will be required.

Just as a portion of a typical student's senior year in college may be occupied with assembling the information and resources needed to apply to a library education program, so a portion of the professional education period probably will be devoted to planning for initial placement. Random reading of lists of positions as they appear regularly in publications mentioned in Appendix C may be a beginning, but a time comes when the potential applicant needs to study those more carefully, relating the job requirements to her or his own competencies and considering whether the work described or the geographic area or the kind of library is the one for which the person is more appropriate and vice versa. The applicant may need to make some mental adjustments, determining whether ideas about salary are realistic in terms of the available positions.

On your own campus you probably will find some assistance at various stages of this process. Faculty members may be willing to advise you about the range of opportunities or to recommend you for or inform you about specific positions. Since their general responsibilities are to all the students, not to an individual, their interest and time may be limited. The school may post announcements of openings, provide copies of journals and papers that include advertisements for positions, or offer seminars or discussions by administrators with responsibility for personnel or placement counselors who may be informative about how to go about the task of finding and getting a position.

Early Opportunities

Some of the most satisfying initial placements occur when students are able to find positions in settings where they are already working. Many libraries and information centers employ students. Although student employment does not guarantee anyone of a future position, the alert student who has performed effectively almost literally has one foot in the door if a beginning professional position opens. You may wish to keep this in mind when seeking a part-time position while enrolled in school.

Another kind of opportunity may be available to those who compete successfully for the various internships or work-study programs available. Typically these also stipulate that the intern should not expect that the experience will lead to the offer of a position, but in reality there often is that possibility. In addition, however, some other research libraries, academic libraries, and other kinds of libraries may have internship programs. The bases on which these are run may vary considerably in terms of formality, their link with library education programs, and the opportunity they offer to the chosen interns. However, since prior experience usually is rated as important by potential employers, the fact that one has acquired such experience is often a value in itself.

Sources of Help

Although there are helpful resources for you when seeking your first professional position, it should be noted here that the initiative and the follow-through of suggestions must be yours. Others may inform, advise, and recommend, but you must decide what you will apply for, whether you can invest in travel for interviews, and whether there are some areas of the country or some kinds of library positions that you will not consider—in short, what investment you are willing to make in your search for a position.

What are some of these resources? And how can you find and use them to your advantage? The Internet provides a variety of valuable resources for job seekers in the library profession. An excellent source of information about Internet resources is the *Guide to Internet Job Searching,* by Margaret Riley Dikel and Frances Roehm, published by the Public Library Association and VGM Career Books. This guide includes a section specifically for library and information sciences, which lists websites, listservs, and bulletin boards. Another excellent source of library employment resources on the Internet is the *Internet Public Library,* a worldwide website maintained at the University of Michigan, with links to academic and professional association listings, searchable databases, compiled guides, mailing lists, and some nonlibrary-specific Internet sites. To access the *Internet Public Library,* connect to www.ipl.org/, their home page, and from there proceed to the "Library Employment" page via the link "Especially for Librarians."

You should also contact the university's or the library school's placement service. You should learn the terms on which it is available, such as whether a fee is charged, and whether service is limited to graduates. If you believe its services are useful, you should use them, without relying exclusively on them. Some placement services provide information about jobs, others handle credentials and submit them to prospective employers, and many perform both of these services. The handling of credentials is a time-consuming task and can represent a great service to the student. In this way, letters of reference can be collected at one time and sent out on request so that you do not have to solicit them repeatedly.

For some positions, usually those in academic libraries or school libraries, and also for entrance to another academic program, you may need your library school transcripts. These usually are handled by the registrar's office for a fee, but it is a good idea for you to find out how to get them as quickly and efficiently as possible, because you may have to provide them with little notice. Official transcripts usually must be sent to a third party, another educational institution, or a prospective employer, not directly to the student or graduate.

Although the university's placement service may be the most important single channel for information and assistance in seeking a position, it may be supplemented with more informal channels. Faculty members, fellow students, bulletin board or other kinds of announcements, and librarians or information scientists among the school's alumni also may provide information.

Some of the various agencies available to assist in placement in general are listed later in this chapter. Information of this kind may become rapidly outdated as the placement scene changes in various parts of the country and as informal means of communication increase. Local library and information science associations may provide assistance in placement, perhaps posting positions at meetings or maintaining a file of positions available.

There are also individuals in the profession who are in key positions to hear about opportunities. They may be placement officers in libraries, staff members of professional associations, or library and information science education faculty members. If they are aware of your needs and interests, they may be able to assist you in finding the kind of position you want. Those who may have encouraged you to enter the profession may be able to provide personal assistance and information. Like the other groups and individuals who may assist, these people are probably better able to do so if they have accurate, current information about the applicant on hand. Providing them with resumes that have been carefully prepared for employers and letting them know what your present status and hopes are can be important moves on your part.

MIDCAREER PLACEMENT

Librarians and information scientists are, on the whole, a fairly mobile group of people. Those with an eagerness to work in different kinds of settings, a strong sense of purpose, and a willingness to take some risks are probably among the most mobile. Even those who stay in one library system may consider their options for other kinds of placement from time to time and may have to use some of the same techniques as they would use if they were changing systems.

Occasionally, advancement or change occurs spontaneously. Your supervisor retires or resigns, and you are promoted to the position. Or work on the committee of a professional association brings you into contact with the director of another library who urges you to accept a position that is open there. You may help develop a new service and then become the person responsible for it.

The Mental Alarm Clock

Ideally, you need a kind of mental alarm clock, keeping track of how long you have been doing the same thing, whether there is still challenge in a job, and what kind of move you should make next to achieve the eventual goal you want. It is usually only in fiction that the unknown person at the fourth desk back is invited to become head of the corporation. In real life, experience needs to be acquired, often in a variety of settings or in a variety of specializations and usually with increasing responsibility, before an employee is chosen to accept a major administrative assignment.

The mental alarm clock also should remind you of the need for current letters of reference, which may be added to your original placement file and which may be much easier to acquire at times when you are not actively seeking a position. Supervisors might write these after an evaluation interview, or colleagues might be asked to write them after completion of some major project.

Some people like to keep their placement files active at all times, in order to be informed of potential positions they may wish to consider. Others may do so only when they are actively seeking a change. In a more casual way, nearly everyone keeps an eye on the announcements of available positions, comparing one's own experience, academic background, and salary with the criteria and benefits offered for other positions. Even a quick review of the announcements of new appointments to positions can keep you informed of classmates, former colleagues, or other acquaintances and of their changes of position, which may in turn suggest the desirability of change for you if your current position has begun to lose its challenge.

There is certainly more likelihood at the midcareer level that an individual will be sought out for a job than there is when he or she is initially employed. The general quality of the person's work, written reports, or activity in professional associations may call an individual to the attention of others. So, at times, the individual may have to decide whether to follow up on an invitation or a suggestion that might be appealing but that has not been anticipated.

Other Reasons for Midcareer Change

Advancement is not the only reason for midcareer changes. A parent's illness, a broken marriage, a desire for travel, or a spouse's new position in another part of the country can occasionally necessitate change. In most cases like these, the individual will have to repeat many of the same steps followed when he or she sought the first position: preparing a resume, reviewing announcements of positions, reactivating a file in the placement service, letting friends and associates know of the plan to move. One difficulty may be that if no position equivalent in salary and responsibility with the former position is available, the person may have to consider accepting one at a lower level or perhaps making a major shift to another kind of library or to somewhat different work. Some prospective employers may be reluctant to employ the person if they consider the person overqualified for the position available, because they think he or she may become dissatisfied or bored in a position that does not provide enough challenge.

One consideration in contemplating a midcareer change is that it is at least twice as easy to get a job when one has a job as it is to get one while unemployed. For that reason it may be a good idea to take a leave of absence rather than resign in order to enjoy a year's travel. A trip to the part of the country where one plans to move can be a reasonable investment if it means it is possible to seek a position and schedule interviews there while still employed elsewhere.

In recent years pressures from government agencies and civil rights groups have resulted in many positions being advertised much more widely than they had been before, but it still is possible to miss seeing announcements of positions that might be appealing. If a midcareer change is being considered for reasons other than those relating directly to the job, some discreet inquiries to several libraries and information centers in the prospective area may stimulate them to send information about openings there.

A somewhat more difficult circumstance can occur when problems with co-workers make a position untenable or when conscience drives a person to resign. At these times the hardest thing to do may be the most necessary: to review the entire situation as objectively as possible, consider as many options for actions as exist, and act on them in a rational, unhurried way. You need also to keep in mind that, in terms of future employment possibilities, it is undoubtedly true that an employer will accept the fact that one situation was untenable and required a drastic move. He or she is likely, however, to look askance at a career record that involves many short-term appointments, and where, according to the applicant, the problem often was the personality of others or unreasonable demands made.

Length of Time on a Job

That raises the question about when to change jobs in a little different way. How long should you be expected to stay on a job? For professional positions the answer would be not less than one year and, more likely, at least two years. In jobs with special responsibility or set terms of appointment, periods of three or five years may be expected. What is important is for the supervisor and the employee to agree on the appropriate length of time, at least in a general way. It may be a good idea for the employee to raise a question about the length of time expected at the time of the interview for the position. But both people need to realize that the timing of a resignation is also important. Leaving just as someone else in the same department is resigning can increase the impact of a resignation, or resigning just as a superior is recuperating from surgery can be almost traumatic. The same consideration and courtesies that are a part of the process of getting a position should be observed when resigning: written notice, adequate time to plan for the change, and a willingness to make the transition as painless as possible.

Midcareer placement offers special challenges and concerns but is basically similar to initial placement. It may be avidly sought or thrust upon the individual, and its timing is often unpredictable. The person who is satisfied and happy with her or his career will consider midcareer change, as will the one who feels dissatisfied with previous positions. Each has special need to be aware of personal strengths, weaknesses, present value to a prospective employer, future goals, and the means of attaining those goals.

AGENCIES ENGAGED IN PLACEMENT ACTIVITIES

In addition to Internet-based employment sources mentioned above, the following list of library placement services is excerpted from the guide prepared for the *Bowker Annual of Library and Book Trade Information* by the Office for Library Personnel Resources of the American Library Association.

Guide to Employment Sources in the Library and Information Professions*

compiled by Maxine Moore,
Office for Human Resource Development and Recruitment
American Library Association

Library Literature Classified ads of library vacancies and positions wanted are carried in many of the national, regional, and state library journals and newsletters. Members of associations can sometimes list "position wanted" ads free of charge in their membership publications. Listings of positions available are regularly found in *American Libraries, Chronicle of Higher Education, College & Research Libraries News, Library Journal,* and *Library Hotline.* State and regional library association newsletters, state library journals, foreign library periodicals, and other types of periodicals carrying such ads are listed in later sections.

Newspapers The *New York Times* Sunday "Week in Review" section carries a special section of ads for librarian jobs in addition to the regular classifieds. Local newspapers, particularly the larger city Sunday editions, such as the *Washington Post, Los Angeles Times,* and *Chicago Tribune,* often carry job vacancy listings in libraries, both professional and paraprofessional. There are many Web-based versions of the newspapers and journals.

---

*Edited and used by permission of the Office for Library Personnel Resources of the American Library Association, updated 2000. For annual updates, see editions of the Bowker Annual Library and Book Trade Almanac or visit www.ala.org/hrdr/guide/joblines.html.

Internet   The many library-related electronic listservs on the Internet often post library job vacancies interspersed with other news and discussion items. A growing number of general on-line job search Internet sites exist; these may include information-related job notices along with other types of jobs. This book includes information on electronic access where available through the individual organizations listed below. A few Internet-related resources are: "Making Short Work of the Job Search," by Marilyn Rosenthal, *Library Journal,* September 1, 1997; "Job Opportunities Glitter for Librarians Who Surf the Net," by A. Paula Azar, *American Libraries,* September 1996; and "Library Jobs and Employment: A Guide to Internet Resources," compiled by Jeffery C. Lee, Texas Woman's University, under What's New & Featured Resources/Clearinghouse for Subject-Oriented Internet Resource Guides (UM/All Guides/Library Employment; J. Lee; v.1.1, 1/29/95), (www.clearinghouse.net). "Jobs on the Net for Librarians," by Janet B. Foster, in *Public Libraries,* v. 38.1, Jan./Feb. 1999, pp. 27–29; and "Riley's Guided Tour: Job Searching on the Net," by Margaret Riley, et al., *Library Journal,* September 15, 1996, pp. 24–27, offer guidance on databases that might lead to library and information-related position listings.

Some library-related job search Web links include:

- Ann's Place—Library Job Hunting Around the World
  www.uic.edu/~aerobin/libjob/libads.html
- Finding Library Jobs on the WWW-TLA NMRT
  http://toltec.lib.utk.edu/~tla/nmrt/libjobs.html
- Career and Job Information
  www.peachnet.edu/galileo/internet/jobs/jobsmenu.html
- Job Opportunities—Librarians and Library Science Net Links
  http://librarians.miningco.com/msubjobs.htm
- Library Jobs Online http://wings.buffalo.edu/sils/alas/usamap
- The Networked Librarian Job Search Guide
  http://pw2.netcom.com/~feridun/nlintro.htm

Library Joblines

Library joblines, or job "hotlines," give recorded telephone messages of job openings in a specific geographical area. Most tapes are changed once a week, although individual listings may sometimes be carried for several weeks. Although the information is fairly brief and the cost of calling is borne by the individual job seeker, a jobline provides a quick and up-to-date listing of vacancies that is not usually possible with printed listings or journal ads.

Most joblines carry listings for their state or region only, although some will occasionally accept out-of-state positions if there is room on the tape. A few will list paraprofessional positions, but the majority of lists are for professional jobs only. When calling the joblines, one might occasionally find a time when the telephone keeps ringing without any answer; this will usually mean that the tape is being changed or there are no new jobs for that period. The classified section of *American Libraries* carries jobline numbers in issues if space permits.

The following joblines are in operation:

JOBLINE SPONSOR	JOB SEEKERS (To Hear Job Listings)
American Association of Law Libraries	312/939–7877
Arizona Department of Library Archives and Public Records	602/275–2325
British Columbia Library Association	604/430–6411
California Library Association	916/447–5627
California School Library Association	650/697–8832
Cleveland (OH) Area Metropolitan Library System Job Listing Service	216/921–4702
Colorado State Library (includes paraprofessional and out-of-state; weekly printed listing sent on receipt of stamps and mailing labels)	303/866–6741 (for printout)
Delaware Division of Libraries (Delaware, New Jersey, and Pennsylvania listings)	800/282–8696 (in-state) 302/739–4748, ext. 165 (out-of-state)
State Library of Florida	904/488–5232 (in-state)
Library Jobline of Illinois (co-sponsored by the Special Libraries Association, Illinois Chapter and Illinois Library Association)	312/409–5986

(continued)

State Library of Iowa   515/281–7574
  (professional jobs in Iowa;
  only during regular business hours)

Kansas State Library Jobline   785/296–3296
  (also includes paraprofessional and
  out-of-state)

Kentucky Job Hotline   502/564–3008
  (24 hours)

Long Island (NY) Library Resources Council Jobline   516/632–6658

Maryland Library Association   410/685–5760

Metropolitan Washington Council   202/962–3712
  of Governments Library Council (D.C.)
  (24 hours)

Michigan Library Association   517/694–7440

Missouri Library Association Jobline   573/442–6590

Mountain Plains Library Association   605/677–5757
  (includes listings for the states of Arizona,
  Colorado, Kansas, Montana, Nebraska,
  Nevada, North and South Dakota, Oklahoma,
  Utah, and Wyoming; also paid listings from
  out-of-region institutions—$10/week per listing)

Nebraska Job Hotline   402/471–4019
                                                  800/307–2665 (in state)

New England Library Jobline   617/521–2815
  (24 hours)

New Jersey Library Association   609/695–2121

New York Library Association   518/432–6952
                                                  800/252–NYLA (in state)

University of North Texas   940/565–2445
  (free 24-hour job hotline listing
  for current students; $20 for former students)

Ohio Library Council   614/225–6999
  (24 hours)

Oklahoma Department of Libraries Jobline   405/522–4747

Pennsylvania Cooperative Job Hotline   717/234–4646
  (sponsored by the Pennsylvania Library

Association; also accepts paraprofessional
out-of-state listings)

Pratt Institute SILS Job Hotline	718/636–3742
University of South Carolina College of Library and Information Science (no geographic restrictions)	803/777–8443
Special Libraries Association	202/234–3632
Special Libraries Association, New York Chapter	212/439–7290
Special Libraries Association, San Andreas–San Francisco Bay Chapter	415/528–7766
Special Libraries Association, Southern California Chapter	626/795–2145
University of Western Ontario Faculty of Communications and Open Learning	519/661–3542

Visit www.ala.org/hrdr/guide/joblines.html to see how employers can list openings.

Specialized Library Associations and Groups

ACCESS, 1001 Connecticut Avenue NW, Suite 838, Washington, D.C. 20036, 202/785–4233; fax 202/785–4212; E-mail: commjobs@aol.com; (www.communityjobs.org): Is a comprehensive national resource on employment, voluntary service, and career development in the nonprofit sector. ACCESS promotes involvement in public issues by providing specialized employment publications and services for job seekers. It serves as a resource to nonprofit organizations on recruitment, diversity, and staff development.

Advanced Information Management, 444 Castro Street, Suite 320, Mountain View, CA 94041, 650/965–7900; fax 650/965–7907; E-mail: aimno.aimusa@juno.com; (www.aimusa.com/hotjobs.html): Placement agency that specializes in library and information personnel. They offer work on a temporary, permanent, and contract basis for both professional librarians and paraprofessionals in the special, public, and academic library marketplace. They supply consultants who can work with special projects in libraries or manage library development projects. They maintain offices in southern California (900 Wilshire Boulevard, Suite 1424, Los Angeles,

CA 90017, 213/489–9800; fax 213/489–9802) as well as in the San Francisco Bay area. There is no fee to applicants.

American Association of Law Libraries Career Hotline, 53 West Jackson Boulevard, Suite 940, Chicago, IL 60604, 312/939–4764: Full listings of all current placement ads are available by fax from the AALL Fax-on-Demand service (call 732/544–5901 and request document 730) or at AALLNET (www.aallnet.org). To place an ad, call the membership co-ordinator at 312/949–4764, ext. 10.

American Libraries, "Career LEADS," c/o American Libraries, 50 East Huron Street, Chicago, IL 60611: Classified job listings published in each monthly issue of *American Libraries* magazine, listing some one hundred job openings grouped by type, plus "Late Job Notices" added near press time, as space and time permit. Contains subsections: "Positions Wanted," "Librarians' Classified," joblines, and regional salary scales. Also contains "ConsultantBase" four times annually. Available on-line at www.ala.org/education/.

American Libraries, ConsultantBase (CBase): An *AL* service that helps match professionals offering library/information expertise with institutions seeking it. Published quarterly, CBase appears in the "Career LEADS" section of the January, April, June, and October issues of *AL.* Rates: $5.50/line—classified; $55/inch—display. Inquiries should be made to LEADS Editor, American Libraries, 50 East Huron Street, Chicago, IL 60611, 800/545–2433 ext. 4211; E-mail: careerleads@ala.org.

American Library Association, Association of College and Research Libraries, 50 East Huron Street, Chicago, IL 60611-2795, 312/280–2513: Classified advertising appears each month in *College & Research Libraries News.* Ads appearing in the print edition of *C&RL News* are also posted to *C&RL NewsNet,* an abridged electronic edition of *C&RL News* (www.ala.org/acrl/c&rlnew2.html).

American Library Association, Office for Human Resource Development and Recruitment (HRDR), 50 East Huron Street, Chicago, IL 60611, 312/280–4279, (www.ala.org/hrdr/placemt.html): A placement service is provided at each annual conference (June or July) and midwinter meeting (January or February). Request job seeker or employer registration forms prior to each conference. Persons not able to attend the conference can register with the service and also can purchase job and job seeker listings sent directly from the conference site. Information is included when requesting registration forms. Handouts on interviewing, preparing a resume, and other job-seeker information are available from ALA HRDR.

In addition to the ALA conference placement center, ALA division national conferences usually include a placement service. See American Libraries "Datebook" for dates of upcoming divisional conferences, since these are not held every year. ALA provides website job postings from *American Libraries, C&RL NewsNet, LITA Job Site,* and its conference placement services (www.ala.org) located in the library education and employment menu page. Also listed is the Library Job Postings on the Internet, compiled by Sarah L. Nesbeitt. See http://webhost.bridgew.edu/snesbeitt/libraryjobs.htm.

American Society for Information Science, 8720 Georgia Avenue, #501, Silver Spring, MD 20910-3602, 301/495–0900; fax 301/495–0810; E-mail: asis@asis.org: There is an active placement service operated at ASIS annual meetings (usually October—locales change). All conference attendees (both ASIS members and nonmembers), as well as ASIS members who cannot attend the conference, are eligible to use the service to list or find jobs. Job listings also are accepted from employers who cannot attend the conference. Interviews are arranged. Throughout the year, current job openings are listed in *ASIS JOBLINE,* a monthly publication sent to all members and available to nonmembers on request with a self-addressed, stamped envelope.

Art Libraries Society/North America (ARLIS/NA), c/o Executive Director, 1550 South Coast Highway, Suite 201, Laguna Beach, CA 92651, 800/892–7547; fax 919/376–3456; E-mail: membership@arlisna.org: Art information and visual resources curator jobs are listed in the *ARLIS/NA UPDATE* (six times a year) and a job registry is maintained at society headquarters. Any employer may list a job with the registry, but only members may request job information. Listings also available on ARLIS-L listserv and website.

Asian/Pacific American Libraries Newsletter, Contact Polychrome Publishing Corp., 4509 North Francisco, Chicago, IL 60626,

773/478–4455; fax 773/478–0786: Quarterly. Includes some job ads. Free to members of Asian/Pacific American Librarians Association.

Association for Educational Communications and Technology, 1800 North Stonelake Drive, Suite Z, Bloomington, IN 47404, 812/335–7675; fax 812/335–7678; E-mail: aect@aect.org: AECT maintains a placement listing on the AECT website (www.aect.org) and provides a placement service at the annual convention; free to all registrants.

Association for Library and Information Science Education, P.O. Box 7640, Arlington, VA 22207, 703/243–8040; fax 703/243–4551; (www.alise.org): Provides placement service at annual conference (January or February) for library and information studies faculty and administrative positions.

Association of Research Libraries, 21 Dupont Circle NW, Washington, D.C. 20036, 202/296–2296; (http://db.arl.org/careers): Job openings at ARL member libraries.

Black Caucus Newsletter, c/o Editor, Rollins College, 1000 Holt Avenue, #2654, Winter Park, FL 32789, 407/646–2677; fax 407/646–2546; E-mail: bcnews@rollins.edu: Lists paid advertisements for vacancies. Free to members; $10/year to others. Published bimonthly by Four-G Publishers, Inc. News accepted continuously. Biographies, essays, books, and reviews of interest to members are invited.

C. Berger Group, Inc., 327 East Gundersen Drive, Carol Stream, IL 60188, 630/653–1115; fax 630/653–1691; E-mail: cberger @cberger.com; (www.cberger.com): CBG conducts executive searches to fill permanent management, supervisory, and director positions in libraries, information centers, and other organizations nationwide. Direct hire and temp-to-hire services also are available. Other employment services include supplying professional and support staff-level temporary workers and contract personnel for short- and long-term assignments in special, academic, and public libraries in Illinois, Indiana, Georgia, Texas, Wisconsin, and other states. In addition, CBG provides library and information management consulting services, as well as direction and staff to manage projects for clients both onsite and offsite.

Canadian Library Association, 200 Elgin Street, Suite 602, Ottawa, ON, Canada K2P 1L5, 613/232–9625; (www.cla.ca): Publishes career ads in

Feliciter magazine. Provides career ads on-line. Operates a "Jobmart" at the annual conference in June.

Carney, Sandoe & Associates, 136 Boylston Street, Boston, MA 02116, 800/225–7986; fax 617/542–9400; E-mail: Jonathan_Ball@Carney Sandoe.com: Is an educational recruitment firm that places teachers and administrators in private, independent schools across the United States and overseas. They have placed more than seven thousand teachers and administrators in independent schools since 1977. CS&A has thousands of positions available in all primary and secondary subjects each year. All fees are paid by the hiring schools. Services are free to the candidate, and teacher certification is not necessary.

Catholic Library Association, 9009 Carter Street, Allen Park, MI 48101; E-mail: cla@vgernet.net: Personal and institutional members of CLA are given free space (thirty-five words) to advertise for jobs or to list job openings in *Catholic Library World* (four/year). Others may advertise. Contact advertising coordinator for rates.

Chinese-American Librarians Association Newsletter, c/o Wichita State University Libraries, Head of Technical Services, Wichita, KS 67260: Job listings in newsletter issued in February, June, October. Free to members.

Council on Library/Media Technicians, Inc., c/o Membership Chair, P.O. Box 52057, Riverside, CA 92517–3057; (http://library.ucr.edu/COLT): COLT information appears bimonthly in *Library Mosaics*. Personal dues/U.S. $35; foreign $60; students $30; institutions/U.S. $60; foreign $85.

Gossage Regan Associates, Inc., 25 West Forty-third Street, New York, NY 10036, 212/869–3348; fax 212/997–1127: An executive search firm specializing in the recruitment of library directors and other library/information handling organization top management. About fifty nationwide searches have been conducted since 1983 for public, academic, and large specialized libraries in all regions of the United States. Salary limitation: $70,000 up.

Independent Educational Services, 1101 King Street, Suite 305, Alexandria, VA 22314, 800/257–5102 or 703/548–9700; fax 703/548–7171; (www.ies search.org): IES is a nonprofit faculty and administrative placement agency for independent elementary and secondary schools across the country. Qualified candidates must possess an M.L.S. degree and some experience in a school setting working with students. Jobs range from assistant librarians and interns to head librarians and rebuilding entire libraries/multimedia centers. Regional offices in Boston and San Francisco.

Labat-Anderson, Inc., 8000 Westpark Drive, #400, McLean, VA 22102, 703/506–9600; fax 703/506–4646: One of the largest providers of library and records management services to the federal government. Supports various federal agencies in twenty-seven states, with many positions located in the Washington, D.C., Atlanta, and San Francisco areas. Resumes and cover letters will gladly be accepted from librarians with an ALA-accredited M.L.S. and records managers, or from applicants with library and/or records management experience, for full- and part-time employment.

The Library Co-Op, Inc., 3840 Park Avenue, Suite 107, Edison, NJ 08820, 732/906–1777 or 800/654–6275; fax 732/906–3562; E-mail: librco@com puserve.com: The company is licensed as both a temporary and permanent employment agency and provides consultants to work in a wide variety of information settings and functions from library moving to database management, catalog maintenance, reference, retrospective conversion, and more. Recent developments include the forming of two new divisions: LAIRD Consulting provides a full range of automation expertise for hardware, software, LANS, and WANS. It is a reseller of INMAGIC software for Windows 95/98 and NT. The second new division is ABCD Filing Services and the hiring of two specialists in space planning.

Library Management Systems, Corporate Pointe, Suite 755, Culver City, CA 90230, 310/216–6436 or 800/567–4669; fax 310/649–6388; E-mail: lms@ix.netcom.com; and Three Bethesda Metro Center, Suite 700, Bethesda, MD 20814, 301/961–1984; fax 301/652–6240; E-mail: lmsdc@ix.netcom.com: LMS has been providing library staffing, recruitment, and consulting to public and special libraries and businesses since 1983. LMS organizes and manages special libraries; designs and implements major projects, including retrospective conversions, automation studies, and records management, etc.; performs high-quality cataloging outsourcing; and furnishes contract staffing to all categories of information centers. LMS has a large database of librarians and library assistants on call for long- and short-term projects and provides permanent placement at all levels.

Library Mosaics, P.O. Box 5171, Culver City, CA 90231, 310/645–4998; (www.librarymosaics.com): Magazine appears bimonthly and will accept listings for library/media support staff positions. However, correspondence relating to jobs cannot be handled.

Medical Library Association, 65 East Wacker Place, Suite 1900, Chicago, IL 60601–7298, 312/419–9094 ext. 29; (www.mlanet.org): *MLA News* (ten issues per year, June/July and November/December combined issues) lists positions wanted and positions available in its "Employment Opportunities" column. The position-available rate is $2.80 per word for advertisements. Up to fifty free words for MLA members plus $2.45 per word over fifty words. Members and nonmembers may rerun ads once in the next consecutive issue for $25. All positions-available advertisements must list a minimum salary; a salary range is preferred. Positions-wanted rates $1.50 per word for nonmembers; $1.25 per word for members with one hundred free words; $1.25 will be charged for each word exceeding one hundred. MLA also offers a placement service at the annual meeting each spring. Job advertisements received for *MLA News* publication are posted to the MLANET Jobline.

Music Library Association, c/o MLA Placement Officer, 1814 Pine Grove Avenue, Colorado Springs, CO 80906–2930, 719/475–1960; E-mail: erebman@library.berkeley.edu; (www.musiclibraryassoc.org): Monthly job list $20/year individuals; $25 organizations. Send to MLA Business Office, P.O. Box 487, Canton, MA 02021, 781/828–8450; fax 781/828–8915; E-mail: acadsvc@aol.com.

Pro Libra Associates, Inc., 6 Inwood Place, Maplewood, NJ 07040, 973/762–0070 or 800/262–0070; E-mail: prolibra-2@mail.idt.net: A multiservice library firm, Pro Libra specializes in personnel placement (permanent and temporary), consulting, management, and project support for libraries and information centers. For more than twenty-four years, it has provided personnel services to catalog, inventory, rearrange, and staff libraries and information centers in corporate, academic, and public institutions.

REFORMA, National Association to Promote Library Service to the Spanish-Speaking, P.O. Box 832, Anaheim, CA 92815–0832: Employers wishing to do direct mailings to the REFORMA membership (nine hundred plus) may obtain mailing labels arranged by zip code for $100. Call 714/738–6383. Job ads also are published quarterly in the *REFORMA Newsletter.* For rate information, call 510/430–2021; E-mail: almag@ mills.edu.

Society of American Archivists, 527 South Wells Street, 5th floor, Chicago, IL 60607–3922, 312/922–0140; fax 312/347–1452; E-mail: info@archivists.org; (www.archivists.org): The *Archival Outlook* is sent to members only six times annually and contains features about the archival profession and other timely pieces on courses in archival administration, meetings, and professional opportunities (job listings). The Online Employment Bulletin is a weekly listing of professional opportunities posted on the website. The *SAA Employment Bulletin* is a bimonthly listing of job opportunities available to members by subscription for $24 per year, and to nonmembers for $10 per issue. Prepayment is required.

Special Libraries Association, 1700 Eighteenth Street NW, Washington, D.C. 20009-2514, 202/234–4700; fax 202/265–9317; E-mail: sla@sla.org; (www.sla.org): SLA maintains a telephone jobline— SpeciaLine, 202/234–4700 ext. 1—which is in operation twenty-four hours a day, seven days a week. Most SLA chapters have employment chairpersons who make referrals for employers and job seekers. Several SLA chapters have joblines. The association's monthly magazine, *Information Outlook,* carries classified advertising. SLA offers an employment clearinghouse and career advisory service during its annual conference held in June. SLA also provides a discount to members using the resume evaluation service offered through Advanced Information Management. A "Guide to Career Opportunities" is a resource kit for $20 (SLA members, $15); "Getting a Job: Tips and Techniques" is free to unemployed SLA members. The SLA Job Bulletin Board, a computer listserv, is organized by Indiana University staff. Subscribe by sending the message—subscribe SLAJOB first name, last name—to listserv@iubvm.ucs.indiana.edu.

TeleSec CORESTAFF, Information Management Division, 11160 Veirs Mill Road, Suite 414, Wheaton, MD 20902, 301/949–4097; fax 301/949–8729; E-mail: library@corestaff.com: Offers a variety of opportunities to start a library career in the Washington, D.C. area, including direct hire, temporary, temp-to-hire, and contract positions. Positions are in the major federal agencies, law firms, corporations, associations, and academic institutions of metropolitan Washington. TeleSec CORESTAFF has been a leader in the staffing industry since its founding in 1948. Check the website for library openings and to register on-line: www.corestaff.com/searchlines/.

Tuft & Associates, Inc., 1209 Astor Street, Chicago, IL 60610, 312/642–8889; fax 312/642–8883: Specialists in nationwide executive searches for administrative posts in libraries and information centers.

Wontawk Gossage Associates, 304 Newbury Street, Boston, MA 02115, 617/867–9209; fax 617/437–9317: Temporary/permanent assignments in the New York, New Jersey, Connecticut, and Boston metropolitan areas in all types of library/information management, professional and support positions, all levels of responsibility, all skills.

State Library Agencies

In addition to the joblines just mentioned, some of the state library agencies issue lists of job openings within their areas. These include: Colorado (weekly, sent on receipt of stamps and mailing labels. Also available via listserv and Access Colorado Library & Information Network [ACLIN], send SASE for access); Indiana (monthly on request, 317/232–3697 or in Indiana area 800/451–6028); Iowa; and Nebraska.

Some state libraries have indicated they have an electronic source that lists job openings, including:

- Arizona and Colorado list out-of-state jobs (www.aclin.org), type JOBLINE as the code
- D.C., Metropolitan Washington Council of Governments Library Council (www.mwcog.org/ic/jobline.html)
- Florida (www.dos.state.fl.us/dlis/jobs.html)
- Georgia (www.public.lib.ga.us/pls/job-bank)
- Idaho (www.lili.org/staff/jobs.html)
- Indiana (www.statelib.lib.in.us/WWW/LDO/POSOP16.HTML)
- Iowa (www.silo.lib.ia.us/)
- Kentucky (www.kdla.state.ky.us/libserv/jobline.htm)
- Louisiana (www.state.lib.la.us/Publications/jobs.htm)
- Massachusetts (www.mlin.lib.ma.us)

- Mississippi (www.dell-2300.mlc.lib.ms.us/home.htm)
- Missouri (http://mosl.sos.state.mo.us/lib-ser/libser.html)
- Montana (http://jsd.dli.state.mt.us/)
- Nebraska (www.nlc.state.ne.us/libjob)
- New Hampshire (www.state.nh.us/nhsl/ljob/index.html)
- North Carolina (http://statelibrary.dcr.state.nc.us/jobs/jobs.htm) lists both professional and paraprofessional library positions
- Oklahoma (www.odl.state.ok.us/fyi/jobline.htm)
- Pennsylvania listserv is maintained by Commonwealth Libraries
- South Carolina via telnet (leo.scsl.state.sc.us, log in as "ebbs") or (www.state.sc.us/jobs/)
- Tennessee (http://toltec.lib.utk.edu/~tla)
- Texas (www.tsl.state.tx.us)
- Virginia (www.lva.lib.va.us)
- Washington (www.statelib.wa.gov)

When vacancy postings are available, state library newsletters or journals will list these, such as: Alabama (*Cottonboll,* quarterly); Alaska (*Newspoke,* bimonthly); Arizona (*Arizona Libraries NewsWeek*); Indiana (*Focus on Indiana Libraries,* eleven times/year); Iowa (*Joblist*); Kansas (*Kansas Libraries,* monthly); Louisiana (*Library Communique,* monthly); Minnesota (*Minnesota Libraries News,* monthly); Nebraska (*NCompass,* quarterly); New Hampshire (*Granite State Libraries,* bimonthly); New Mexico (*Hitchhiker,* weekly); Tennessee (*TLA Newsletter,* bimonthly); Utah (*Directions for Utah Libraries,* monthly); and Wyoming (*Outrider,* monthly).

Although they may not have formal placement services, many state library agencies will refer applicants informally when vacancies are known to exist. The following states primarily make referrals to public libraries only: Alabama, Arizona, Arkansas, California, Louisiana, Pennsylvania, South Carolina (institutional also), Tennessee, Utah, Vermont, and Virginia.

Those who refer applicants to all types of libraries are: Alaska, Delaware, Florida, Georgia, Hawaii, Idaho, Kansas, Kentucky, Maine, Maryland, Mississippi, Montana, Nebraska, Nevada (largely public and academic), New Hampshire, New Mexico, North Carolina, North Dakota, Ohio, Pennsylvania, Rhode Island, South Dakota, Vermont, West Virginia (on Pennsylvania Jobline, public, academic, special), and Wyoming.

The following state libraries post library vacancy notices for all types of libraries on a bulletin board: California, Connecticut, Florida, Georgia, Hawaii, Illinois, Indiana, Iowa, Kentucky, Nevada, New Jersey, New York, Ohio, Oklahoma, Pennsylvania, South Carolina, South Dakota, Utah, and Washington. Addresses of the state agencies are found in the *Bowker Annual* or *American Library Directory.*

State and Regional Library Associations

State and regional library associations often will make referrals, run ads in association newsletters, or operate a placement service at annual conferences, in addition to the joblines sponsored by some groups. Referral of applicants when jobs are known is done by the following associations: Arkansas, Delaware, Hawaii, Louisiana, Michigan, Minnesota, Nevada, Pennsylvania, South Dakota, Tennessee, and Wisconsin. Although listings are infrequent, job vacancies are placed in the following association newsletters or journals when available: Alabama (*Alabama Librarian,* seven times/year); Alaska (*Newspoke,* bimonthly); Arizona (*Newsletter,* ten times/year); Arkansas (*Arkansas Libraries,* six times/year); Connecticut (*Connecticut Libraries,* eleven times/year); Delaware (*Delaware Library Association Bulletin,* three times/year); District of Columbia (*Intercom,* eleven times/year); Florida (*Florida Libraries,* six times/year); Indiana (*Focus on Indiana Libraries,* eleven times/year); Iowa (*Catalyst,* six times/year); Kansas (*KLA Newsletter,* six times/year); Minnesota (*MLA Newsletter,* six issues/bimonthly); Mountain Plains (*MPLA Newsletter,* bimonthly, lists vacancies and position-wanted ads for individuals and institutions); Nebraska (*NLAQ*); Nevada (*Highroller,* four times/year); New Hampshire (*NHLA Newsletter,* six times/year); New Jersey (*NJLA Newsletter,* ten times/year); New Mexico (shares notices via *State Library's Hitchhiker,* weekly); New York (*NYLA Bulletin,* ten times/year); Ohio (*ACCESS,* monthly); Oklahoma (*Oklahoma Librarian,* six issues/year); Oregon (*OLA Hotline,* twenty-four times/year); Rhode Island (*RILA Bulletin,* six times/year); South Carolina (*News and Views*); South Dakota (*Book Marks,* bimonthly); Tennessee (*TLA Newsletter*); Vermont (*VLA News,* ten issues/year); Virginia (*Virginia Libraries,* quarterly); and West Virginia (*West Virginia Libraries,* six times/year).

The following associations have indicated some type of placement service or job help/search service, although it may only be held at annual conferences: Alabama, California, Connecticut, Georgia, Idaho, Indiana, Iowa, Kansas, Kentucky, Louisiana, Maryland, Massachusetts, New England, New Jersey, New York, North Carolina (biennial), Ohio, Oregon, Pacific Northwest, Pennsylvania, South Dakota, Southeastern, Tennessee, Texas, Vermont, Wisconsin, and Wyoming.

These associations have indicated they have an electronic source for job postings and/or a voice jobline:

- Alabama (http://allaonline.home.mindspring.com *and* allaon line@mindspring.com)
- California (www.cla-net.org/html/jobline.html)
- Connecticut (www.lib.uconn.edu/cla)
- Illinois (www.ila.org)
- Kansas (http://skyways.lib.ks.us/KLA/helpwanted/) no charge to list job openings
- Michigan (www.mla.lib.mi.us)
- Minnesota (www.lib.mankato.msus.edu/)
- Missouri (www.mlnc.com/~mla)
- Nebraska (www.nlc.state.ne.us/libjob/libjob.html)
- New Hampshire (www.state.nh.us/nhsl/ljob.htm)
- New Jersey Library Association (www.njla.org)
- Ohio (www.olc.org/jobline.html)
- Oklahoma (www.state.ok.us/~odl/fyi/jobline.htm *or* E-mail: bpetrie@oltn.odl.state.ok.us)
- Oregon (www.olaweb.org)
- Pacific Northwest Library Association (PNLA) listserv PNLA-L includes job postings in the PNLA region in addition to postings on other library issues. Send—subscribe PNLA-L, your name—to list serv@wln.com *or* listserv@idbsu.idbsu.edu
- Texas (www.txla.org/jobline/jobline.txt)
- Virginia (www.vla.org)
- Wisconsin (www.wla.lib.wi.us/wlajob.htm)

The following associations have indicated they have no placement service at this time: Colorado, Middle Atlantic Regional Library Federation, Minnesota, Mississippi, Montana, Nebraska, Nevada, New

Mexico, North Dakota, Oklahoma, Utah, and West Virginia. State and regional association addresses are found in the *Bowker Annual*.

Library and Information Studies Programs

Library and information studies programs offer some type of service for their current students as well as alumni. Most schools provide job hunting and resume-writing seminars. Many have outside speakers representing different types of libraries or recent graduates relating career experiences. Faculty or a designated placement officer offers individual advising services or critiquing of resumes. Of the ALA-accredited library and information studies programs, the following handle placement activities through the program: Alabama, Albany, Alberta, British Columbia, Buffalo (annually compiles graduate biographical listings), Dalhousie, Dominican, Drexel, Hawaii, Illinois, Kent, Kentucky, Louisiana, McGill, Missouri (College of Education), Pittsburgh (Department of Library and Information Science only), Pratt, Puerto Rico, Queens, Rhode Island, Rutgers, St. John's, South Carolina, Syracuse, Tennessee, Texas-Austin, Toronto, UCLA, Western Ontario, Wisconsin-Madison, and Wisconsin-Milwaukee.

The central university placement center handles activities for the following schools: California-Berkeley (alumni) and Emporia. However, in most cases, faculty in the library school still will do informal counseling regarding job seeking.

In some schools, the placement services are handled in a cooperative manner; in most cases the university placement center sends out credentials while the library school posts or compiles the job listings. Schools utilizing one or both sources include: Alabama, Albany, Alberta, Arizona (School of Information Resources and Library Science maintains an E-mail list: jobops@listserv.arizona.edu); Buffalo, Catholic, Dominican, Florida State, Indiana, Iowa (fee for students and recent alumni is $25/year and includes job bulletins and a service that mails references and vitas to employers), Kent State, Long Island, Maryland, Michigan, Montreal, North Carolina Central, North Carolina at Chapel Hill, North Carolina-Greensboro, North Texas, Oklahoma, Pittsburgh, Queens, St. John's, San Jose, Simmons, South Florida, Southern Connecticut, Southern Mississippi, Syracuse, Tennessee, Texas Woman's, Washington, Wayne State, and Wisconsin-Milwaukee. In sending out placement credentials, schools vary as to whether they distribute these free, charge a general registration fee, or request a fee for each file or credential sent out.

Those schools that have indicated they post job vacancy notices for review but do not issue printed lists are: Alabama, Alberta, Arizona, British Columbia, Buffalo, Catholic, Clark Atlanta, Dalhousie, Drexel, Florida State, Hawaii, Illinois, Indiana, Kent State, Kentucky, Long Island, Louisiana, Maryland, McGill, Missouri, Montreal, North Carolina Central, North Carolina at Chapel Hill, North Carolina-Greensboro, Oklahoma, Pittsburgh, Puerto Rico, Queens, Rutgers, St. John's, San Jose, Simmons, South Carolina, South Florida, Southern Mississippi, Syracuse (general postings), Tennessee, Texas Woman's, Toronto, UCLA, Washington, Wayne State, Western Ontario, and Wisconsin-Madison.

In addition to job vacancy postings, some schools issue printed listings, operate joblines, have electronic access, or provide database services:

- Albany (listserv@cnsibm.albany.edu to subscribe; *Job Placement Bulletin* free to SISP students)
- Alberta (www.bcla.bc.ca/jobs/index.html)
- Arizona (send subscription message to: listserv@listserv.arizona.edu)
- British Columbia (uses BCLA Jobline, 604/683–5354 or 800/661–1445; uses BCLA jobpage at www.bcla.bc.ca/jobs/index.html)
- Buffalo (job postings for alumni: sils-l@listserv.acsu.buffalo.edu; for students: ubmls-l@listserv.acsu.buffalo.edu)
- California-Berkeley (Career Center 510/642–5207)
- Clarion (www.clarion.edu/student/career/jobs/index.htm)
- Dalhousie (listserv for Atlantic Canada jobs, send message to mailserv@ac.dal.ca)
- Dominican (*Placement News* every two weeks, free for six months following graduation: $15/year for students and alumni; $25 to others)
- Drexel (www.cis.drexel.edu/placement/placement.html)
- Emporia (weekly bulletin for school, university, public jobs; separate bulletin for special; $42/six months; Emporia graduates $21/six months)
- Florida State
- Hawaii

- Illinois (in partnership with Indiana and Washington, free on-line placement JOBSearch database available on campus and via access through telnet alexia.lis.uiuc.edu; login: jobs; password: Urbaign; or http://carousel.lis.uiuc.edu/~jobs)
- Indiana (www.slis.indiana.edu/cfdocs/slisjobs)
- Iowa ($15/year for registered students and alumni: www.uiowa.edu/homepage/employers/index.html)
- Kentucky (www.uky.edu/CommInfoStudies/SLIS/jobs.htm)
- Maryland (listserv@umdd.umd.edu to subscribe)
- Michigan (www.si.umich.edu/jobfinder)
- Missouri (www.coe.missouri.edu)
- North Carolina at Chapel Hill (E-mail: listproc@ils.unc.edu to subscribe *or* http://ils.unc.edu/ils/web/listservs.html)
- Oklahoma
- Pittsburgh (www.sis.pitt.edu/~lsdept/libjobs.htm)
- Pratt (free to students and alumni for full-time/part-time professional positions only)
- Rhode Island (monthly, $7.50/year)
- Rutgers (www.scils.rutgers.edu or scils-jobs@scils.rutgers.edu to subscribe)
- Simmons (www.simmons.edu/gslis/jobline.html; operates the New England Jobline, which announces professional vacancies, 617/521–2815)
- South Carolina (www.libsci.sc.edu/career/job.htm)
- South Florida (in cooperation with the ALIS organization)
- Southern Connecticut (www.scsu.ctstateu.edu; printed listing twice a month, mailed to students/alumni free)
- St. John's (send notices to: libis@stjohns.edu *or* fax 718/990–2071; lists job postings for United States, Canada, and abroad)
- Syracuse (lists selected jobs on-line through electronic mail to students)
- Texas-Austin (free to students and alumni for one year following graduation, Weekly Placement Bulletin, listserv $16/six months, $28/one year, mail $26/six months or $48/year, Texas Jobs Weekly, $16/six months or $28/year, (www.gslis.utexas.edu/~careers)
- Texas Woman's (www.twu.edu/o-cs/home.html)
- Toronto (www.fis.utoronto.ca/resources/jobsite)

- Washington (send notices to slis@u.washington.edu)
- Western Ontario (www.fims.uwo.ca/lis/employment.html) resources; to list positions call 519/661–2111 ext. 8495
- Wisconsin-Madison (now sends listings from Wisconsin and Minnesota to Illinois for JOBSearch)
- Wisconsin-Milwaukee (listserv@slis.uwm.edu to subscribe; www.slis.uwm.edu/MLIS_Jobs/MLIS_Job_Links.htm)

Employers often will list jobs with schools only in their particular geographical area; some library schools will give information to nonalumni regarding their specific locales, but they are not staffed to handle mail requests and advice is usually given in person. Schools that have indicated they will allow librarians in their areas to view listings are: Alabama, Albany, Alberta, Arizona, British Columbia, Buffalo, California-Berkeley, Catholic, Clarion, Clark Atlanta, Dalhousie, Dominican, Drexel, Emporia, Florida State, Hawaii, Illinois, Indiana, Iowa, Kent State, Kentucky, Louisiana, Maryland, McGill, Michigan, Missouri, Montreal, North Carolina Central, North Carolina at Chapel Hill, North Carolina-Greensboro, Oklahoma, Pittsburgh, Pratt, Puerto Rico, Queens, Rhode Island, Rutgers, Simmons, San Jose, South Carolina, South Florida, Southern Connecticut, Southern Mississippi, St. John's, Syracuse, Tennessee, Texas-Austin, Texas Woman's, Toronto, UCLA, University of North Texas, Washington, Wayne State, Western Ontario, Wisconsin-Madison, and Wisconsin-Milwaukee. A list of accredited program addresses and phones can be requested from ALA or found in the *Bowker Annual*. Individuals interested in placement services of other library education programs should contact the schools directly.

Federal Employment Information Sources

Consideration for employment in many federal libraries requires establishing civil service eligibility. Although the actual job search is your responsibility, the Office of Personnel Management (OPM) has developed the "USAJOBS" website (www.usajobs.opm.gov) to assist you along the way. The website also has an On-line Resume Builder feature for job seekers to create on-line resumes specifically designed for applying for federal jobs.

OPM's Career America Connection is at 912/757–3000 or 202/606–2700, TDD service at 912/744–2299, for "USAJOBS by Phone." This system provides current worldwide federal job opportunities, salary and employee benefits information, special recruitment messages, and more. You also can record your request to have application packages, forms, and other employment-related literature mailed to you. This service is available twenty-four hours a day, seven days a week.

USA Jobs "Touch Screen" Computer, is a computer-based system utilizing touch screen technology. These kiosks, located throughout the nation in OPM offices, federal office buildings, and other locations, allow you to access current worldwide federal job opportunities, on-line information, and more. Another website for federal jobs is www.fed world.gov/ jobs/jobsearch.html.

Applicants should attempt to make personal contact directly with federal agencies in which they are interested. This is essential in the Washington, D.C., area where over half the vacancies occur. Most librarian positions are in three agencies—Army, Navy, and Veterans Administration.

There are some "excepted service" agencies that are not required to hire through the usual OPM channels. Although these agencies may require the standard forms, they maintain their own employee selection policies and procedures. Government establishments with positions outside the competitive civil service include: Board of Governors of the Federal Reserve System; Central Intelligence Agency; Defense Intelligence Agency; Department of Medicine and Surgery; Federal Bureau of Investigation; Foreign Service of the United States; General Accounting Office; International Monetary Fund; Judicial Branch of the Government; Legislative Branch of the Government; Library of Congress; National Science Foundation; National Security Agency; Organizations of American States; Pan American Health Organization; Tennessee Valley Authority; United Nations Secretariat; U.S. Mission to the United Nations; U.S. Nuclear Regulatory Commission; U.S. Postal Service; World Bank and IFC.

The Library of Congress, the world's largest and most comprehensive library, is an excepted-service agency in the legislative branch and administers its own independent merit selection system. Job classifications, pay, and benefits are the same as in other federal agencies, and qualification requirements generally correspond to those used by the U.S. Office of Personnel Management. The library does not use registers, but announces vacancies as they become available. A separate application must be submitted for each vacancy announcement. For most professional positions, announcements are widely distributed and open for a minimum period of thirty days. Qualification requirements and ranking criteria are stated on the vacancy announcement. The Library of Congress Human Resources Operations Office is located in the James Madison Memorial Building, 101 Independence Avenue SE, Washington, D.C. 20540, 202/707–5620.

Additional General and Specialized Job Sources

Affirmative Action Register, 8356 Olive Boulevard, St. Louis, MO 63132, 314/991–1335 or 800/537–0655; E-mail: aareeo@concentric.net; (www.aar-eeo.com): The goal is to "provide female, minority, handicapped, and veteran candidates with an opportunity to learn of professional and managerial positions throughout the nation and to assist employers in implementing their Equal Opportunity Employment programs." Free distribution of monthly bulletin is made to leading businesses, industrial and academic institutions, and more than four thousand agencies that recruit qualified minorities and women, as well as to all known female, minority, and handicapped professional organizations, placement offices, newspapers, magazines, rehabilitation facilities, and more than eight thousand federal, state, and local governmental employment units with a total readership in excess of 3.5 million (audited). Individual mail subscriptions are available for $15 per year. Librarian listings are found in most issues and are sent free to libraries on request.

The *Chronicle of Higher Education* (published weekly, breaks in August and December), 1255 Twenty-third Street NW, Suite 700, Washington, D.C. 20037, 202/466–1055; fax 202/296–2691: Lists a variety of library positions each week, including administrative and faculty jobs. Job listings are searchable by specific categories, keywords, or geographic locations at chronicle.com/jobs.

Academic Resource Network On-Line Database (ARNOLD), 4656 West Jefferson, Suite 140, Fort Wayne, IN 46804: This World Wide Web interactive database assists faculty, staff, and librarians to identify partners for exchange or collaborative research (http://arnold.snybuf.edu).

School Libraries: School librarians often find that the channels for locating positions in education are of more value than the usual library ones, e.g., contacting county or city school superintendent offices. Other sources include university placement offices that carry listings for a variety of school system jobs. A list of commercial teacher agencies may be obtained from the National Association of Teachers' Agencies, c/o G.A. Agency, 524 South Avenue East, Cranford, NJ 07016–3209, 908/272–2080; fax 908/272–2962; (www.jobsforteachers.com).

Overseas

Opportunities for employment in foreign countries are limited, and immigration policies of individual countries should be investigated. Employment for Americans is virtually limited to U.S. government libraries, libraries of U.S. firms doing worldwide business, and American schools abroad. Library journals from other countries will sometimes list vacancy notices. Some persons have obtained jobs by contacting foreign publishers or vendors directly. Non-U.S. government jobs usually call for foreign language fluency. The Librarian Job Postings (http://bubl.ac.uk/news/jobs) is a listing of U.S. and foreign jobs collected by the Bulletin Board for Libraries.

Council for International Exchange of Scholars (CIES), 3007 Tilden Street NW, Suite 5M, Washington, D.C. 20008–3009, 202/686–7877; E-mail: cies1@ciesnet.cies.org; (www.cies.org): Administers U.S. government Fulbright awards for university lecturing and advanced research abroad; usually ten to fifteen awards per year are made to U.S. citizens who are specialists in library or information sciences. In addition, many countries offer awards in any specialization of research or lecturing for which specialists in library and information science may apply. Lecturing awards usually require university or college teaching experience. Several opportunities exist for professional librarians as well. Applications and information may be obtained, beginning in March each year, directly from CIES. Worldwide application deadline is August 1.

Department of Defense, Dependents Schools (DODDS), Recruitment Unit, 4040 North Fairfax Drive, Arlington, VA 22203–1634, 703/696–3068; fax 703/696–2697; E-mail: recruitment@odeddodea.edu: Overall management and operational responsibilities for the education of dependent children of active duty U.S. military personnel and DOD civilians who are stationed in foreign areas. Also responsible for teacher recruitment. For complete application brochure, write to above address. The latest copy of *Overseas Opportunities for Educators* is available and provides information on educator employment opportunities in more than 167 schools worldwide. The schools are operated on military installations for the children of U.S. military and civilian personnel stationed overseas.

International Schools Services, P.O. Box 5910, Princeton, NJ 08543, 609/452–0990: Private, not-for-profit organization founded in 1955 to serve American schools overseas, other than Department of Defense schools. These are American, international elementary and secondary schools enrolling children of business and diplomatic families living abroad. ISS services to overseas schools include recruitment and recommendation of personnel, curricular and administrative guidance, purchasing, facility planning, and more. ISS also publishes a comprehensive directory of overseas schools and a bimonthly newsletter, *NewsLinks,* for those interested in the intercultural educational community. Information regarding these publications and other services may be obtained by writing to the above address.

Peace Corps, 1111 Twentieth Street NW, Washington, D.C. 20526: Volunteer opportunities exist for M.A./M.S. or B.A./B.S. in library science with one year of related work experience. Two-year tour of duty; U.S. citizens only. Living allowance, health care, transportation, and other benefits provided. Write for additional information and application or call 800/424–8580.

Search Associates, P.O. Box 922, Jackson, MI 49204–0922, 517/768–9250; fax 517/768–9252; (www.search-associates.com): A private organization comprised of former overseas school directors who organize about ten recruitment fairs (most occur in February) to place teachers, librarians, and administrators in around four hundred independent, K–12 American/international schools around the world. These accredited schools, based on the American model, range in size from fewer than forty to more than four thousand students and serve the children of diplomats and businesspeople from dozens of countries. They annually offer highly attractive personal and professional opportunities for experienced librarians.

Overseas—Exchange Programs

International Federation of Library Associations and Institutions (IFLA) Secretariat, c/o Koninklijkebibliotheek, Pn Willem-Alexanolerhof S, 2595

BE The Hague, Netherlands, fax 31–70–3834827; E-mail: ifla@nlc-bnc.ca or (www.ifla.org): Most exchanges are handled by direct negotiation between interested parties. A few libraries have established exchange programs for their own staff. In order to facilitate exchange arrangements, the *IFLA Journal* (issued January, March, May, July, October/November) lists persons wishing to exchange positions outside their own country. All listings must include the following information: full name, address, present position, qualifications (with year of obtaining), language, abilities, preferred country/city/library, and type of position.

LIBEX Bureau for International Staff Exchange, Thomas Parry Library, University of Wales Aberystwyth (formerly Information and Library Studies Library), Llanbadarn Fawr, Aberystwyth, Ceredigion SY23 3AS, Wales, United Kingdom, tel. 01970–622417; fax 01970–622190; E-mail: parrylib@aber.ac.uk *or* (www.aber.ac.uk/~tplwww/libex.html): Assists in exchanges for British librarians wishing to work abroad and for librarians from the United States, Canada, E.E.C. countries, Commonwealth, and other countries who wish to undertake exchanges.

Using Information Skills in Nonlibrary Settings

A great deal of interest has been shown in using information skills in a variety of ways in nonlibrary settings. These jobs are not usually found through the regular library placement sources, although many library and information studies programs are trying to generate such listings for their students and alumni. Job listings that do exist may not call specifically for "librarians" by that title, so ingenuity may be needed to search out jobs where information management skills are needed.

Some librarians are working on a freelance basis by offering services to businesses, alternative schools, community agencies, legislators, etc.; these opportunities are usually not found in advertisements but are created by developing contacts and publicity over a period of time. A number of information brokering business firms have developed from individual freelance experiences. Small companies or other organizations often need "one-time" service for organizing files or collections, bibliographic research for special projects, indexing or abstracting, compilation of directories, and consulting services. Bibliographic networks and on-line database companies are using librarians as information managers, trainers, researchers, systems and database analysts, on-line services managers, etc. Jobs in this area are sometimes found in library network newsletters or data processing journals.

Librarians can be found working in law firms as litigation case supervisors (organizing and analyzing records needed for specific legal cases); with publishers as sales representatives, marketing directors, editors, and computer services experts; and with community agencies as adult education coordinators, volunteer administrators, grants writers, etc.

Classifieds in *Publisher's Weekly* and *The National Business Employment Weekly* may lead to information-related positions. One also might consider reading the Sunday classified ad sections in metropolitan newspapers in their entirety to locate descriptions calling for information skills but under a variety of job titles.

Burwell Enterprises, 5619 Plumtree Drive, Dallas, TX 75252–4928, 281/537–9051; fax 281/537–8332; E-mail: burwellinfo@burwellinc.com: The *Burwell World Directory of Information Brokers* is an annual publication that lists information brokers, freelance librarians, independent information specialists, and institutions that provide services for a fee. There is a minimal charge for an annual listing and the Burwell Directory On-line is searchable free on the Internet at www.burwellinc.com. Print and CD-ROM versions are available. Also published is a bimonthly newsletter, *Information Broker,* which includes articles by, for, and about individuals and companies in the fee-based information field; book reviews; calendar of upcoming events; and issue-oriented articles. A bibliography and other publications on the field of information brokering also are available.

Classifieds can be obtained through The Association of Independent Information Professionals, which was formed for individuals who own and operate for-profit information companies. Contact AIIP Headquarters at 212/779–1855.

A growing number of publications are addressing opportunities for librarians in the broader information arena:

- "You Can Take Your MLS Out of the Library," by Wilda W. Williams, *Library Journal,* Nov. 1994, pp. 43–46.

- *Opening New Doors: Alternative Careers for Librarians,* edited by Ellis Mount, Washington, D.C.: Special Libraries Association, 1993, provides profiles of librarians who are working outside libraries.
- *Extending the Librarian's Domain: A Survey of Emerging Occupation Opportunities for Librarians and Information Professionals,* by Forest Woody Horton, Jr., Washington, D.C., 1994, explores information job components in a variety of sectors.

Classifieds in Careers in Electronic Information, by Wendy Wicks, 1997, 184 pp., and *Guide to Careers in Abstracting and Indexing,* by Wendy Wicks and Ann Marie Cunningham, 1992, 126 pp., are available from National Federation of Abstracting Information Services, 1518 Walnut Street, Philadelphia, PA 19102, 215/893–1561, (www.nfais.org); E-mail: nfais@nfais.org. The American Society of Indexers, 11250 Roger Bacon Drive, Suite 8, Reston, VA 20190-5202, 703/234–4147, fax 703/435–4390, info@asindexing.org, (www.ASIndexing.org), has a number of publications that would be useful for individuals who are interested in indexing careers.

Temporary/Part-Time Positions

Working as a substitute librarian or in temporary positions may be considered to be an alternative career path as well as an interim step while looking for a regular job. This type of work can provide valuable contacts and experience. Organizations that hire library workers for part-time or temporary jobs include:

Advanced Information Management, 444 Castro Street, Suite 320, Mountain View, CA 94041, 650/965–7900 or 900 Wilshire Boulevard, Suite 1424, Los Angeles, CA 90017, 213/489–9800.

C. Berger Group, Inc., 327 East Gundersen Drive, Carol Stream, IL 60188, 630/653–1115 or 800/382–4222.

Gossage Regan Associates, Inc., 25 West Forty-third Street, New York, NY 10036, 212/869–3348 and Wontawk Gossage Associates, 304 Newbury Street, Boston, MA 02115, 617/867–9209; Information Management Division, 1160 Veirs Mill Road, Suite 414, Wheaton, MD

20902, 301/949–4097; The Library Co-Op, Inc., 3840 Park Avenue, Suite 107, Edison, NJ 08820, 732/906–1777 or 800/654–6275.

Library Management Systems, Corporate Pointe, Suite 755, Culver City, CA 90230, 310/216–6436 or 800/567–4669 and Three Bethesda Metro Center, Suite 700, Bethesda, MD 20814, 301/961–1984.

Pro Libra Associates, Inc., 6 Inwood Place, Maplewood, NJ 07040, 201/762–0070; part-time jobs are not always advertised but often are found by canvassing local libraries and leaving applications.

JOB HUNTING IN GENERAL

Wherever information needs to be organized and presented to patrons in an effective, efficient, and service-oriented fashion, the skills of librarians can be applied, whether or not they are in traditional library settings. However, it will take considerable investment of time, energy, imagination, and money on the part of an individual before a satisfying position is created or obtained in a conventional library or another type of information service. Usually, no one method or source of job hunting can be used alone.

Public and school library certification requirements often vary from state to state; contact the particular state library agency for such information. Certification requirements are summarized in *Certification of Public Librarians in the United States,* fourth edition, 1991, from the ALA Office for Human Resource Development and Recruitment. A summary of school library/media certification requirements by state is found in *Requirements for Certification of Teachers, Counselors, Librarians, and Administrators for Elementary and Secondary Schools,* published annually by the University of Chicago Press. "School Library Media Certification Requirements: 1994 Update" by Patsy H. Perritt, also provides a compilation in *School Library Journal,* June 1994, pp. 32–49. State supervisors of school library media services also may be contacted for information on specific states.

Civil service requirements either on a local, county, or state level often add another layer of procedures to the job search. Some civil service jurisdictions require written and/or oral examinations; others assign a ranking based on a review of credentials. Jobs are usually filled from the top candidates on a qualified list of applicants. Since the exams are held only at certain times and a variety of jobs can be filled from a single list of applicants (e.g., all Librarian I positions regardless of type of function), it is important to check whether a library in which one is interested falls under civil service procedures.

If one wishes a position in a specific subject area or in a particular geographical location, remember those reference skills to ferret information from directories and other tools regarding local industries, schools, subject collections, etc. Directories such as the *American Library Directory, Subject Collections, Directory of Special Libraries and Information Centers,* and *Directory of Federal Libraries,* as well as state directories or directories of other special subject areas, can provide a wealth of information for job seekers. Some state employment offices will include library listings as part of their job services department.

Some students have pooled resources to hire a clipping service for a specific time period in order to get classified librarian ads for a particular geographical area. Interesting sources in the library literature are "Employment and Job Search," by Charlie Fox, *Library Mosaics,* v. 10–3, May/June 1999, pp. 5–19; "Have I Got A Job For You," by Joni R. Roberts, *Library Mosaics,* v. 10–3, May/June 1999, pp. 14–15; and "We're Honored That You Applied Here," by Terry Ballard, *Information Today,* v. 15–2, Feb. 1998, p. 42. Another Internet source is www.careerpath.com.

For information on other job-hunting and personnel matters, contact the ALA Office for Human Resource Development and Recruitment, 50 East Huron Street, Chicago, IL 60611 (www.ala.org/hrdr).

SALARIES, STATUS, TENURE, RETIREMENT, AND RELATED BENEFITS

Recently, there has been greater emphasis placed on the benefits offered by a particular position than on its salary. These benefits may include hospitalization and other medical insurance, retirement plans, housefinding assistance, and aid in negotiating for the purchase of a home. For initial appointment and for a change of positions, it is important to determine the various benefits of the job and to set up a way to compare the different programs at different libraries or information centers.

Salaries

In thinking about salaries it is useful to have an idea of the salary range for people with similar qualifications in similar positions; you must recognize, however, that no two people are exactly alike or exactly comparable in those terms. Sources of information about reasonable expectations may be placement counselors, surveys of salaries such as the one for beginning positions that has appeared annually in *Library Journal,* and advertisements for positions in which a salary range is given.

In evaluating a salary, it may be useful to compare it with the actual take-home pay received during each pay period. The pattern of pay periods can be important, too; if you are accustomed to being paid every other week, you may find it difficult to adjust to monthly payments or vice versa. The amount of state income tax withheld and such other deductions as dues in a staff association or union can have considerable effect on the ratio of take-home pay to actual earnings. In comparing positions in two different locations, the relative costs of living should be considered. If a car is required for the job but not supplied by the library or information center, if circumstances require a lengthy commute, or if evening hours require additional amounts for food or transportation, you should figure those costs as deductions from the salary offered.

It is wise to obtain a salary schedule, if available, and to note your place on it and possible opportunities for advancement. Information about when and how salary increments are made should be obtained as early as possible. In fact it is a good idea to verify all impressions and benefits information before actually committing yourself to a permanent position.

Actual salaries of librarians and information scientists are difficult to pinpoint because of the diversity of settings in which these people work. Regional differences may mean that very different salaries are paid for the same position. Although a beginning librarian may start in the low $20,000s per year, the director of a large academic library may earn more than $100,000.

One sector of library employment where good data are available is that of new graduates from schools accredited by the American Library Association. Information is provided annually in *Library Journal,* which reports salary by type of placement and region.

Another way to discover current regional salaries is to peruse job announcements in periodicals such as *Library Journal* or *American Libraries.*

Listed below are selected announcements from the January 2001 issue of the ALA's "Career Leads."

- *Access Services Librarian* for a small university library: $35,000–$38,000
- *Executive Director* of a division of the American Library Association; starting salary negotiable: $60,000–$75,000
- *Director of Library Services* for a research library: $54,000–$64,000
- *Full-Time Children's Librarian or Trainee* for a public library in New York; starting salary: about $29,050
- *Librarian I* for a public library in Florida (MLS only): $30,540–$45,285
- *Librarian II* for the same library system in Florida: $33,557–$49,760

A list of librarian salary surveys is available from the ALA Office for Library Personnel Resources, 50 East Huron, Chicago, IL 60611.

According to the *Occupational Outlook Handbook,* a publication of the U.S. Bureau of Labor Statistics, salaries of librarians vary according to the individual's qualifications and the type, size, and location of the library. Librarians with primarily administrative duties often have greater earnings.

Median annual earnings of librarians in 1998 (the latest figures currently available) were $38,470. The middle 50 percent earned between $30,440 and $48,130. The lowest 10 percent earned less than $22,970 and the highest 10 percent earned more than $67,810.

Median annual earnings in the industries employing the largest numbers of librarians in 1997 were as follows:

- Elementary and secondary schools: $38,900
- Colleges and universities: $38,600
- Local government, except education and hospitals: $32,600

The average annual salary for all librarians in the federal government in nonsupervisory, supervisory, and managerial positions was $56,400 in 1999.

Status and Tenure

Salaries may be only one small part of the benefits package. The employee's status and that of other employees in the library and information services of an institution also should be verified. The most frequently discussed benefits issue related to academic libraries is whether faculty status is accorded to professional employees in the library. Usually, this status means that individual employees are placed on salary scales comparable to, or equal to, those of the teaching faculty. Academic rank (professor, associate professor, and so on) also may be assigned; requirements for advancement and tenure may be set for faculty library staff members on a basis similar to that for other faculty. The individual considering appointment in an academic library should find out what the present status of librarians is, whether there are any efforts underway that are likely to change it, and what the prospects are for advancement or simply for continuing an appointment at that institution.

There may be other aspects to status. Customarily, you should expect to be employed at the level for which you are academically prepared, with experience also a part of the consideration. This assumes that, as a professional person, you will receive a professional appointment, unless exceptional circumstances lead you to accept a different kind of assignment. In that case you should aim at a clear understanding of your responsibilities in terms of remaining in the position a set period of time and of the employer's position in regard to possible future opportunity or change of status.

Tenure, as generally related to personnel matters, refers to the benefit that ensures that the individual will be retained permanently in the current position or in a comparable one, except for extremely unusual causes. These causes may be conviction of crime, exceptional loss of revenue to the employing institution, thus requiring drastic reduction of personnel, or similar situations. Tenure customarily is granted only after a specified period of employment, since it commits the institution to a long-term agreement in which the employee is relatively free to leave, but the institution is not as free to dismiss the employee. In academic libraries and school libraries, tenure is a customary benefit, but it must be earned. It should be remembered that tenure usually is offered in terms of general employment, not in terms of a specific position. Thus, in a school library, tenure may protect the librarian when curtailment of funds reduces the library program, but the librarian may have to accept a position as a teacher in order to remain in a professional position in the school district.

The benefit of tenure is virtually unknown in special libraries, where competition for excellence may be deliberately encouraged, with every staff member attempting to show her or his value and with job security an uncommon benefit for all personnel. Some public libraries have a kind of tenure system in which staff members are considered permanent after a set period of time, but it is subject to the same kinds of pressures as exist in other, more formal systems.

Retirement

The retirement plans of various libraries and information centers vary. There are also policies about the terms of retirement that should be known to all employees. For example, is early retirement—before age sixty-five, for example—encouraged? Is it possible? Is there an age for mandatory retirement? Is there provision for retirement based on disability? Are there any benefits available to retired staff members—for example, use of the library's facilities and staff? Although it may seem that questions about retirement are of major interest to older staff members only, everyone should be interested in them, not only because eventually they may seem more relevant to the individual, but also because the library's attitude toward its retired staff members may be an indication of the value and interest it associates with all employees.

Social Security retirement benefits usually are available to public employees now. Working people contribute a portion of their salaries (withheld at the time they are paid); employers also contribute a similar amount, with both parts going toward a fund that will provide retirement benefits to the individual. Other benefits associated with Social Security are provisions for allotments to surviving spouses and children in the event of an employee's death. In most instances the amount to be received from Social Security at the time of retirement is so small that other retirement plans must be implemented.

To provide the kind of financial security most people will need in retirement, many employers require participation in plans similar to Social Security. The employee contributes a set amount of her or his income; the employing institution supplements that with a matching or similar amount. Sometimes the employing institution may pay all of an employee's contribution to the plan, but such other benefits as salary may be proportionally lower.

State retirement or pension plans, municipal employee plans, and such national plans as Teachers Insurance and Annuity Association include large numbers of employees, thus usually ensuring good financial management of the pension funds. The national plans may offer the additional advantage of permitting an individual to remain in the same plan without remaining at the institution. The chief values of these retirement plans are that they enforce regular saving, provide a supplement in the employer's contributions, and provide for some mobility without loss of benefits.

Related Benefits

Other kinds of benefits may be numerous and difficult to determine in value. Credit union membership may be open to library personnel, providing another encouragement to savings and possible source of loans. Hospitalization and other kinds of medical health insurance also may be offered, sometimes with the employer paying a major part of the premiums. The different kinds of health insurance, the arrangements for payment of premiums, and the length of time before becoming eligible for benefits are important matters to be checked, especially when changing positions.

Some employers offer free or reduced tuition. At an institution of higher education, the benefit may be extended to the employee's children or spouse, either at that institution or at a comparable one. The provision of full or partial reimbursement for tuition for courses taken is more common in other kinds of libraries. If there are stipulations to these educational benefits, it is usually the employee's responsibility to meet whatever requirements are set.

Other kinds of fringe benefits may be reimbursement of travel expenses for professional meetings or conferences, payment of an individual's dues in professional associations, or provision of such assets as professional books or periodicals. One unstated benefit may be the access to resources that a position in a library or information center offers its employees. Their personal research interests may be served in this way; they also may avoid fees charged for using some collections.

The category of benefits is broad, including more than those discussed here. Decisions about benefits are personal decisions, but information about their availability should be generally well publicized. You have an obligation to yourself to find out about the benefits available and to use them intelligently.

CHAPTER 5

THE FUTURE OF THE
INFORMATION PROFESSIONS

Management of information is a growth profession. Governments, universities, corporations, and schools are acquiring and using information at greater rates than at any time in the past. The advent of electronic publishing finds individuals able to connect with vast databases and the Internet from their home offices through a computer. Telecommunications make it possible to transmit data and E-mail to colleagues instantaneously.

However, the average individual is overwhelmed by so much easily obtained information. Business and universities could not cope with the masses of information available to them without the services of a skilled information manager. Regardless of the type of institution in which information professionals choose to work—libraries, information centers, archives, or database firms—the need for their skills will continue to increase.

Developing models of libraries of the future includes an emphasis on technology to dissolve limitations and enhance the idea of the learning society. It seems most likely that the future of the library is best imagined from the point of view of the user rather than any of the structural components that might be assembled to provide service. From this vantage point the evolution from paper library to automated library to electronic library is simply a continuum of better mechanisms to respond to end-user needs. What drives librarians to maintain professional domination over information provision to users, however, is not merely the mastery of technology or the facilitation of collaborative partnerships, but the librarians' vision of equal access for all.

Digitization, as exemplified by the Library of Congress National Digital Library Program, will change the way we store and retrieve information. For example, the Library of Congress has digitized millions of items including Revolutionary War maps, handwritten drafts of the Declaration of Independence and the Gettysburg Address, and personal papers of the first twenty-three U.S. presidents. In 1996 more than *one million* transactions per day were taking place via the Library of Congress's electronic services. The oversight of this scope of preservation is simply one of the ways in which the role of information professionals has been changing over the last decade.

The simultaneous development of digitized information storage and delivery *and* a growing and pervasive commitment to a learning society positions library and information professionals to activate technology. While we, as a profession, can imagine users shifting from working with librarians providing service from a library to working with librarians who facilitate access from a terminal, can our users? A simple analogy might do. Over the last decade or so, shopping on-line has escalated as a way in which many people acquire goods. For these fairly focused consumers the experience of browsing, looking, and interacting is less important than expediency. Yet traditional stores continue to provide goods to consumers who may have no phone, may have no credit cards, or may simply be disinclined to place convenience over other objective experiences. Will we see the demise of the marketplace as it is configured today? Most likely not, as many individuals view purchasing as a more complex set of activities than simply acquiring merchandise. In much the same way there are information seekers who *see the library as place* as important as obtaining discrete information.

There are so few public spaces that any may enter, that as suburban sprawl and the hectic demands of daily life impose higher levels of stress and aimlessness, the library will remain a cultural institution in which vast amounts of information are stored in an orderly, timeless fashion.

This is not to say that the evolution of the virtual library will not continue, nor that it will not engage a larger and larger market share of users, but that the library as a physical place where individuals go for human assistance will co-exist over the next twenty years or so.

The future of careers in the information profession is one of excitement, integration of new technologies, and the inspired commitment to preserve the record of human achievement and make it available to all. Other important concerns for information professionals are discussed below.

INTELLECTUAL FREEDOM

One of the proudest traditions of American librarianship has been its defense of intellectual freedom. Simply stated, this usually has been closely related to issues about selection and use of library materials, requiring that libraries have the freedom to make available to their users all kinds of materials, without regard for the pressures that may be exerted by special-interest groups to limit the provision of books, journals, and other materials to the library's users.

In more recent years concern for an individual's privacy has led to new problems of intellectual freedom. Any agency that is concerned with information and its acquisition and storage is likely to collect material that is of special value to some outside agency. This may be the result of research that could be extremely valuable to a corporation other than the one that initiated it, or it could be information on the reading (or at least the book-borrowing) habits of an individual about whom others wish information. There is a conflict between the long tradition of libraries and information centers to provide information freely and their obligations to serve the agency that funds or controls them and to preserve the rights of individuals to privacy.

One may expect that these complicated questions will become more complex and numerous in time. It is important that those entering careers in the information fields have clear principles of their own and clear understandings of the requirements of their work and of the need to deal with these issues in a reasonable, ethical way.

SOCIAL RESPONSIBILITY AND
INFORMATION EQUITY

Although there has never been a question that libraries and information centers have a responsibility to society, the term *social responsibility* has come in recent years to have special significance. It refers to the need to provide fair service to all, to employ people on an equitable basis, to represent among employees minority groups, and to take stands on public issues. In some instances there can be confusion and conflict between the responsibility to defend intellectual freedom and the one to defend social responsibility, because the former suggests openness to the provision of all information and the latter suggests emphasis on a particular point of view.

An interesting example of this conflict occurs, for example, when selection of materials for children's collections deals with the problem of how females and males are presented in media for children. The idea that girls are weak while boys are strong or that girls are stay-at-homes while boys are adventurers is repugnant to most people. Children's books and other media that suggest or firmly state that idea are numerous, and those who believe in presentation of truly fair and equal gender roles have strongly supported removing biased media from library collections. There is strong support for close cooperation with publishers and producers to eliminate such stereotyped presentations. There is similarly strong support for the idea that such pressure is in violation of intellectual freedom, closely allied with, if not identical to, censorship.

Also, as electronic information resources become more available, librarians and information scientists have taken a strong stance that "information equity" is a central social responsibility. This means expanding library services to include Internet access and working to ensure that information is electronically accessible to all.

Social responsibility also can affect the employment policies of a library or information center; recent emphasis on providing opportunities for members of minority groups sometimes has resulted in preferential hiring practices. Here, too, there are conflicting arguments. One point of view is that such preference is only fair in light of the fact that for generations minorities (and women) were the targets of discrimination in many personnel practices and policies. The other view is that preference itself is inappropriate and the only way to achieve fairness is to hire according to level of competence.

OPPORTUNITIES IN THE FUTURE

There are two major ways that a field can expand its opportunities: by expanding the scope of its area or special competence and by demonstrating the need for more people to enter it. In an ideal society there could hardly be enough or too many information professionals.

Librarianship and information science have been successful in expanding the scope of their fields. Electronic resources, for example, are now regularly administered by librarians who have developed the interest and skill to deal with them. The application of computer technology to most library operations has not only made services such as bibliographic searching and complicated interlibrary loans possible, but it also has expanded the field so that individuals with computer science, management information systems (MIS), or systems analysis education have been attracted to the profession. Another way the field has grown is through the expansion of its clientele. For example, the availability of information to business executives and that group's recognition of the value of good informational programs have been factors in the development of many special libraries.

Effects of Society and Technology

Although it is always tempting to speculate about what information professionals may be doing in the future, it is important to keep in mind that, as always, librarianship will be affected by society and technology. If, as some people predict, the school of the future will really be an individual workstation where a student will connect to the Internet, it might seem that there will be no need for a librarian at the neighborhood school. However, there may be several information professionals via the Internet at another location organizing the information the student receives. Their skills may be generally quite similar to those of today's school library media specialists.

Diversity of Opportunities

One long-range prediction seems safe: the diversity of opportunities available in librarianship and information science will continue. Although some specializations within the two fields may not be required, the need for further specialization in other areas probably will increase the need for both basic and continuing education. Increased specialization may limit the opportunities for individuals to move from one area of librarianship or information science to another and may make it necessary for those entering the fields to decide earlier what their long-range areas of interest are. This also can have an obvious effect on the educational programs in the fields, since the development of new specialties may send people back to school for further training.

Another factor is the success that librarians and information scientists may enjoy in the private sector. Although this part of the economy has traditionally employed only a small minority of librarians, if freelance opportunities are increased in number and if the special competencies of librarians and information scientists are utilized in more large industrial or commercial enterprises, the number of information professionals needed will dramatically increase.

The Individual's Future

Most of us, however, are more concerned with our own individual futures, say, for the next ten or fifteen years, than we are with that of the profession as a whole. Some specializations, such as science librarians, systems administrators, or youth services librarians, continue to be in especially short supply.

The person entering librarianship as a profession is torn between trying to prepare in as general a way as possible to be sure to find a position, and stressing her or his special background because it may be important to find the kind of position for which the person is best suited. This creates a kind of tension that may result in an individual's missing some opportunities because her or his general background is comparable to that of many others who are seeking the same kind of opportunity. Also, some specialties may not be in urgent demand, so their value is more limited.

The Nature of the Job

In some ways examining the fields of librarianship and information science is like examining an elephant the way the legendary three blind men did. To the man at one end, the elephant was all tail; to the one in the middle, the elephant was like a wall; the third, feeling the tusks, had still a different impression. Information scientists who work in the management area of their field may be unaware of the skills needed in dealing with people— skills that are still needed by those in librarianship who are interpreting reference questions, explaining the use of the library, or testifying before the city council to persuade the public to support a library bond issue. A librarian working with children in a school library media center may wonder why he or she ever needed to master a foreign language or learn cataloging, while a colleague in the processing center of the same school system could not survive without those skills.

Planning, managing, supervising, and administering complex library systems are the work of librarians and information scientists, but these are still fields where there is room for people who want to be in an entrepreneurial role, too. Perhaps best of all is the fact that one person may be able to move from one sort of specialty to another in the course of a career. The person who wants to continue in direct public service may do so, and another who aspires to major administrative responsibilities can move in that direction, while a third, perhaps with additional education acquired in the course of full-time work, can move into a new specialty.

Is It for *Your* Future?

Basically, if you are convinced that the information professions make up a field in which you can find personal and professional satisfaction, there will be many varied job opportunities. It is important for you to assess your own abilities, prepare yourself with the educational requirements, and use as touchstones individuals in the field who may be able to advise you about possible opportunities that would be appropriate for you. What those individuals may not be knowledgeable about is the general outlook for positions, so you should also review placement literature, noting which skills or specialties are among the most sought and whether positions are in the kinds of libraries and localities where you want to work. Openness to experience, willingness to try new places to live or new kinds of specialties, commitment to librarianship, and such personal qualities as a certain toughness and interest in others and sense of purpose—these are as likely to be important in the future as they have been in the past for those in the information professions.

LIBRARY AND INFORMATION SCIENCE PROFESSIONAL ORGANIZATIONS

It is natural for individuals who share common interests and common work to form organizations that may serve to exchange information, encourage education, and, in general, improve the status of those who make up its membership. Librarianship and information science certainly have their share of these. There are regional and state groups as well as national and international ones. In some instances large cities have their own clubs or chapters of some larger association. Of greater interest, in general, are those that are composed chiefly of individual members. Some directory information about them follows. Readers who wish a more thorough introduction to the variety of groups, including information about when they were founded, what their goals are, and other details may consult the latest edition of the *Encyclopedia of Associations,* a publication of Gale Research Corporation, or the *Bowker Annual Library and Book Trade Almanac,* a publication of R. R. Bowker. Readers also should conduct an Internet search to find additional organizations and sources of information.

An E-mail or letter via post to each association asking for further information on the area of library and information science for which they provide services can bring you more data on specialized careers.

The American Association for Artificial Intelligence
445 Burgess Drive
Menlo Park, CA 94025-3442
www.aaai.org/

The American Association for Artificial Intelligence (AAAI) is a non-profit scientific society devoted to advancing the scientific understanding of the mechanisms underlying thought and intelligent behavior and their embodiment in machines. AAAI also aims to increase public understanding of artificial intelligence, improve the teaching and training of AI practitioners, and provide guidance for research planners and funders concerning the importance and potential of current AI developments and future directions.

The American Association of Law Libraries
www.washlaw.edu/

The American Indian Library Association
www.nativeculture.com/lisamitten/aila.html

AILA is an affiliate of the American Library Association (ALA).

The American Library Association
50 East Huron
Chicago, IL 60611

ALA Washington Office
1301 Pennsylvania Avenue NW, Suite 403
Washington, D.C. 20004
E-mail: ala@ala.org
www.ala.org/

The Association provides opportunities for the professional development and education of librarians, library staff, and trustees; it promotes continuous, lifelong learning for all people through library and information services of all types.

The American Medical Informatics Association
4915 St. Elmo Avenue, Suite 401
Bethesda, MD 20814
E-mail: mail@mail.amia.org
www.amia.org/

The mission of the American Medical Informatics Association is to advance the field by fostering innovation and scientific exchange, educating professionals and the public, and influencing decision and policy makers regarding the use of information in health and biomedicine.

American Society for Information Science
1320 Fenwick Lane, Suite 510
Silver Spring, MD 20910
www.asis.org/

Provides education and networking opportunities to information professionals (including librarians, webmasters, information specialists, educators, researchers, publishers, information center managers) in organizations around the world. Bridges the gap between information science research and information services practice.

The American Theological Library Association
250 South Wacker Drive, Suite 1600
Chicago, IL 60606-5834
E-mail: atla@atla.com
www.atla.com/

Membership is open to any person who is engaged in professional library or bibliographic work in theological or religious fields, or who has an interest in the literature of religion, theological librarianship, and the purposes and work of the association.

The Art Libraries Society of North America
329 March Road, Suite 232
Box 11
Kanata, Ontario K2K 2E1
Canada
E-mail: arlisna@igs.net
www.arlisna.org/

Through its conferences, publications, awards, and its website, ARLIS/NA provides resources and services for the worldwide arts information community.

The Association of Canadian Archivists
P.O. Box 2596, Station D
Ottawa, Ontario K1P 5W6
Canada
E-mail: aca@magmacom.com
http://aca.archives.ca/index.htm

The ACA has a fourfold focus: 1) to provide leadership for everyone engaged in the preservation of Canada's documentary heritage, 2) to encourage awareness of archival activities and developments and the importance of archives to modern society, 3) to advocate the interests and needs of professional archivists before government and other regulatory agencies, and 4) to further the understanding and cooperation among members of the Canadian archival system and other information and culture-based professions.

The Association of Canadian Map Libraries and Archives
c/o Visual and Sound Archives Division
National Archives of Canada
395 Wellington Street
Ottawa, Ontario K1A 0N3
Canada
www.sscl.uwo.ca/assoc/acml/acmla.html

ACMLA actively serves as the representative professional group for Canadian map librarians, cartographic archivists, and others interested in geographic information in all formats.

Association of Christian Librarians
P.O. Box 4
Cedarville, OH 45314
E-mail: info@acl.org
www.acl.org/

ACL is an organization of evangelical Christian academic librarians that promotes the professional and spiritual growth of its members and provides service to the academic library community worldwide.

The Association for Information and Image Management
AIIM International
1100 Wayne Avenue, Suite 1100
Silver Spring, MD 20910
E-mail: aiim@aiim.org
www.aiim.org/

The core focus of AIIM is to help users connect with suppliers who can help them apply document and content technologies to improve their internal processes.

The Association for Information Systems
AIS Administrative Office
P.O. Box 2712
Atlanta, GA 30301-2712
www.aisnet.org/

AIS is a professional organization whose purpose is to serve academics specializing in information systems. AIS's mission is to advance knowledge of how the use of information technology can lead to improved organizational performance and individual quality of work life.

The Association of Jewish Libraries
15 East Twenty-sixth Street, Room 1034
New York, NY 10010
E-mail: ajl@jewishbooks.org
http://aleph.lib.ohio-state.edu/www/ajl.html

AJL is dedicated to supporting the production, collection, organization, and dissemination of Judaic resources and library/media/information services in the United States, Canada, and more than twenty-three other countries.

The Association of Research Libraries
21 Dupont Circle, Suite 800
Washington, D.C. 20036
E-mail: arlhq@arl.org.
http://arl.cni.org/

ARL is an organization comprising the leading research libraries in North America. Its mission is to shape and influence forces affecting the future of research libraries in the process of scholarly communication. ARL programs and services promote equitable access to and effective use of recorded knowledge in support of teaching, research, scholarship, and community service.

Canadian Health Libraries Association
P.O. Box 94038
3324 Yonge Street
Toronto, Ontario M4N 3R1
Canada
E-mail: chla@inforamp.net
www.med.mun.ca/chla/

The CHLA's mission is to improve health and health care by promoting excellence in access to information.

Canadian Library Association
328 Frank Street
Ottawa, Ontario K2P 0X8
Canada
www.cla.ca/

The Canadian Library Association provides services to a diverse group of individuals and organizations involved with, or interested in, library or information sciences.

CAUSE, The Association for the Management of Information Technology in Higher Education
4840 Pearl East Circle, Suite 302E
Boulder, CO 80301
www.cni.org/docs/CAUSE.html

CAUSE is the association for the management of information technology in higher education. CAUSE's mission is to promote more effective planning, management, and evaluation of all information technologies in colleges and universities, and to help individual member representatives develop as professionals in the field of higher education technology management.

International Association of Aquatic and Marine Science Libraries
    and Information Centers
c/o Library
Harbor Branch Oceanographic Institution, Inc.
5600 US 1 North
Fort Pierce, FL 34946
http://siolib-155.ucsd.edu/iamslic/

IAMSLIC is an association of individuals and organizations interested in aquatic and marine information science. The association provides a forum for exchange and exploration of ideas and issues of mutual concern.

The International Association of Music Information Centres
    (IAMIC) Secretary
Stiftgasse 29, A-1070
Vienna, Austria
www.iamic.ie/

Music Information Centres are open to the public and have extensive resources to offer. In addition to large libraries of sheet music and sound archives, some centres maintain up-to-date collections of biographical and research material, many issue publications and recordings, and all serve as a focus of musical activity.

The International Association of School Librarianship
Dept. 962, Box 34069
Seattle, WA 98124-1069
E-mail: iasl@rockland.com
www.hi.is/~anne/iasl.html

The mission of IASL is to provide an international forum for those interested in promoting effective school library media programs as viable instruments in the educational process.

The International Association of Technological University Libraries
http://educate.lib.chalmers.se/IATUL/index.html

IATUL was founded in Düsseldorf, Germany, in 1955 as an international forum for the exchange of ideas relevant to librarianship in technological universities throughout the world.

The International Council on Archives
www.ica.org

The International Federation for Information Processing
9, Hofstraße 3, A-2361 Laxenburg
Austria
E-mail: ifip@ifip.or.at
www.ifip.or.at/

IFIP is a nongovernmental, nonprofit umbrella organization for national societies working in the field of information processing.

The International Federation for Systems Research
www.sea.uni-linz.ac.at/ifsr/

The overall purpose of the federation is to advance cybernetic and systems research and systems applications and to serve the international systems community.

The Medical Library Association
65 East Wacker Place, Suite 1900
Chicago, IL 60602-4805
E-mail: info@mlahq.org
www.mlahq.org/

The association is dedicated to improving the quality and leadership of the health information professional to foster the art and science of health information services.

The Music Library Association
6707 Old Dominion Drive, Suite 315
McLean, VA 22101
E-mail: mla-web@musiclibraryassoc.org
www.musiclibraryassoc.org/

The MLA is the professional organization in the United States devoted to music librarianship and to all aspects of music materials in libraries.

The National Association of Government Archives and Records
    Administrators
http://witloof.sjsu.edu/peo/allorgs/orgs.html

The National Association of State Information Resource Executives
167 West Main Street, Suite 600
Lexington, KY 40507-1324
E-mail: nasire@amrinc.net
www.nasire.org/

NASIRE represents state chief information officers and information resource executives and managers from the fifty states, six United States territories, and the District of Columbia.

Progressive Librarians Guild
P.O. Box 2203, Times Square Station
New York, NY 10108
http://libr.org/PLG/

PLG is committed to providing a forum for the open exchange of radical views on library issues; conducting campaigns to support progressive and democratic library activities locally, nationally, and internationally; supporting activist librarians as they work to effect changes in their own libraries and communities; and bridging the artificial and destructive gaps between school, public, academic, and special libraries, and between public and technical services.

The Public Library Association
(A division of the American Library Association)
50 East Huron Street
Chicago, IL 60611
E-mail: pla@ala.org
www.pla.org/

PLA's purpose is to advance the development and effectiveness of public library service and public librarians.

REFORMA, The National Association to Promote Library Services
    to the Spanish Speaking
P.O. Box 832
Anaheim, CA 92815-0832
E-mail: reforma1971@hotmail.com
http://clnet.ucr.edu/library/reforma/

REFORMA is committed to the improvement of the full spectrum of library and information services for the approximately thirty million Spanish-speaking and Latino people in the United States.

The Society of American Archivists
527 South Wells Street, 5th Floor
Chicago, IL 60607-3922
E-mail: info@archivists.org
www.archivists.org/

Membership in the SAA is open to those who are or have been engaged in the custody or control of records, archives, or private papers, or who wish to support the objectives of the society.

The Special Libraries Association (SLA)
1700 Eighteenth Street NW
Washington, D.C. 20009-2514

E-mail: sla@sla.org
www.sla.org/

The mission of the SLA is to advance the leadership role of its members
in putting knowledge to work for the benefit of decision makers in corporations, government, the professions, and society; as well as to shape
the destiny of our information and knowledge-based society.

A list of this kind only suggests the diversity of interests represented by
the larger associations. Most of these groups have sections, divisions, or
chapters—smaller groups that are concerned with one area of specialization or one geographic region. Additional library and information sciences
associations are listed in the *Bowker Annual Library and Book Trade
Almanac* and on the Web.

EDUCATIONAL PROGRAMS IN LIBRARIANSHIP AND INFORMATION SCIENCE

The number and variety of educational programs in librarianship and information science can add to the confusion you may feel when considering whether to enroll in a program of professional or technical education in one of these areas. Although local institutions may offer programs, it is desirable to get a sense of what the range of opportunity is and to learn as much as possible about the various programs in operation at different institutions. Sometimes, career counseling offices or libraries may provide catalogs from the various educational programs; if these are current, they can be quite useful. However, some directory assistance is necessary to provide addresses of programs so that you may write for further information. It should be noted that the directories mentioned here are usually in the process of revision and that, if and when later editions are available, they should always be preferred, since their information is more current.

The American Library Association Standing Committee on Library Education is the best central source for information on different levels of library and information science education. The following items can be obtained by contacting:

American Library Association
    Standing Committee on Library Education
    50 East Huron Street
    Chicago, IL 60611
    www.ala.org

- *Guidelines for Choosing a Library and Information Studies Graduate Program*
- *Financial Assistance for Library Education*
- *Requirements for Admission and a Degree*
- *Joint Degrees Offered by Library Education Programs*
- *Graduate Library Education Programs: Descriptive Information*
- *Library Technical Assistant Programs*
- *Undergraduate Programs in Library Education*
- *Graduate Library Education Programs* (revised semi-annually)

The last item lists master's, advanced study, and doctoral-level programs in the United States and Canada. Because study in an accredited program of library and information science is the most common way to gain the professional credential needed for information work, the accredited programs and their addresses are listed below. Contact schools in which you are interested for complete information on the course of study and financial aid opportunities.

LIBRARY AND INFORMATION SCIENCE PROGRAMS ACCREDITED BY THE AMERICAN LIBRARY ASSOCIATION

United States

Alabama

The University of Alabama
School of Library and Information Studies
Box 870252
Tuscaloosa, AL 35487-0252
www.slis.ua.edu
Master of Library and Information Studies
Distance education opportunities: Birmingham, Gadsden, Huntsville, Mobile

Arizona

University of Arizona
School of Information Resources and Library Science
1515 East First Street
Tucson, AZ 85719
E-mail: sirls@u.arizona.edu
www.sir.arizona.edu
Master of Arts
Distance education opportunities: Internet

California

San Jose State University
School of Library and Information Sciences
One Washington Square
San Jose, CA 95192-0029
E-mail: office@wahoo.sjsu.edu
www.slisweb.sjsu.edu
Master of Library and Information Science
Distance education opportunities: Fresno, Fullerton, Pasadena, Sacramento,
San Diego, San Francisco, San Marcos, Sonoma, and Stockton
Two-way interactive video, Web-supported

University of California, Los Angeles
Department of Information Studies
Graduate School of Education & Information Studies
2320 Moore Hall
Mailbox 951521
Los Angeles, CA 90095-1521
www.is.gseis.ucla.edu
Master of Library and Information Science

Colorado

See Kansas, Emporia State University

Connecticut

Southern Connecticut State University
School of Communication, Information, and Library Science
Department of Library Science and Instructional Technology
501 Crescent Street
New Haven, CT 06515
E-mail: libscienceit@scsu.ctstateu.edu
www.SouthernCT.edu/~brownm/
Master of Library Science and others
Distance education opportunities: On-line MLS

District of Columbia

The Catholic University of America
School of Library and Information Science
Washington, D.C. 20064
E-mail: cua-slis@cua.edu
www.cua.edu/www/lsc/
Master of Science in Library
Distance education opportunities: Fairfax, Norfolk, Richmond

Florida
Florida State University
School of Information Studies
Tallahassee, FL 32306-2100
www.fsu.edu/~lis
Master of Science
Master of Arts
Distance education opportunities: Internet

University of South Florida
School of Library and Information Science
4202 East Fowler Avenue, CIS 1040
Tampa, FL 33620-7800
www.cas.usf.edu/lis/
Master of Arts
Distance education opportunities: Ft. Lauderdale, Ft. Myers, Gainesville, Lakeland, Miami, Orlando, Palm Beach, Sarasota
Distance education opportunities: Internet

Georgia
Clark Atlanta University
School of Library and Information Studies
300 Trevor Arnett Hall
223 James P. Brawley Drive
Atlanta, GA 30314
www.cau.edu
Master of Science in Library Service

Hawaii
University of Hawaii
Library and Information Science Program
2550 The Mall
Honolulu, HI 96822
E-mail: lischair@yahoo.com
www.hawaii.edu/slis/
Master of Library and Information Science
Distance education opportunities: Hawaii Interactive Television System (HITS) limited to islands of Hawaii, Kauai, Lanai, Maui, Molokai, and Oahu (six sites)

Illinois
Dominican University
Graduate School of Library and Information Science
7900 West Division Street

River Forest, IL 60305
E-mail: gslis@email.dom.edu
www.dom.edu/academic/gslishome.html
www.stkate.edu (College of St. Catherine)
Master of Library and Information
Distance education opportunities: Chicago, Northbrook, Vernon Hills, IL;
St. Paul, MN

University of Illinois at Urbana-Champaign
Graduate School of Library and Information Science
Library and Information Science Building
501 East Daniel Street
Champaign, IL 61820
www.alexia.lis.uiuc.edu
Master of Science
Distance education opportunities: Internet

Indiana

Indiana University
School of Library and Information Science
Main Library 012
1320 East Tenth Street
Bloomington, IN 47405-3907
iuslis@indiana.edu
www.slis.indiana.edu
Master of Library Science
Master of Information Science

Iowa

University of Iowa
School of Library and Information Science
3087 Library
The University of Iowa
Iowa City, IA 52242-1420
www.uiowa.edu/~libsci
Master of Arts
Distance education opportunities: various sites within Iowa

Kansas

Emporia State University
School of Library and Information Management
P.O. Box 4025
Emporia, KS 66801

E-mail: sliminfo@emporia.edu
www.slim.emporia.edu
Master of Library Science
Distance education opportunities: Denver, CO; Overland Park, KS; Albuquerque, NM; Portland, OR; Salt Lake City, UT
Videotape, statewide teleconferencing system, Internet

Kentucky

University of Kentucky
College of Communications and Information Studies
School of Library and Information Science
502 King Library Building S
Lexington, KY 40506-0039
www.uky.edu/CommInfoStudies/SLIS/
Master of Arts
Master of Science in Library Science
Distance education opportunities: Covington, Elizabethtown, Highland Heights, Louisville, KY; Cincinnati, OH
Interactive video, Internet

Louisiana

Louisiana State University
School of Library and Information Science
267 Coates Hall
Baton Rouge, LA 70803
E-mail: slis@lsu.edu
Master of Library and Information
Distance education opportunities: Alexandria, Eunice, Lake Charles, Monroe, New Orleans, Shreveport
Two-way interactive video, Internet (selected courses)

Maine

See South Carolina, University of South Carolina

Maryland

University of Maryland
College of Information Studies
4105 Hornbake Library Building
College Park, MD 20742-4345
E-mail: clisumpc@umdacc.umd.edu
www.clis.umd.edu
Master of Library Science

Massachusetts
Simmons College
Graduate School of Library and Information Science
300 The Fenway
Boston, MA 02115-5898
www.simmons.edu/programs/gslis
Master of Science
See also Rhode Island, University of Rhode Island

Michigan
University of Michigan
School of Information
304 West Hall Building
550 East University Avenue
Ann Arbor, MI 48109-1092
E-mail: si.admissions@umich.edu
www.si.umich.edu
Master of Science in Information

Wayne State University
Library and Information Science Program
106 Kresge Library
Detroit, MI 13348202
www.lisp.wayne.edu
Master of Library and Information Science
Distance education opportunities: Farmington, Flint, Grand Rapids, Kalamazoo, Lansing, Saginaw

Minnesota
See Illinois, Dominican University
See Texas, University of North Texas

Mississippi
University of Southern Mississippi
School of Library and Information Science
Box 5146
Hattiesburg, MS 39406-5146
www-dept.usm.edu/~slis
Master of Library and Information Science
Distance education opportunities: Interactive video sites, Internet: whole and partial on-line courses

Missouri
University of Missouri-Columbia
School of Information Science and Learning Technologies
303 Townsend Hall
Columbia, MO 65211
E-mail: sisltnfo@coe.missouri.edu
www.coe.missouri.edu/~sislt
Master of Arts
Distance education opportunities: Kansas City, Springfield, St. Louis
Internet

Nebraska
See Kansas, Emporia State University

New Hampshire
See Rhode Island, University of Rhode Island

New Jersey
Rutgers University
School of Communication, Information, and Library Studies
4 Huntington Street
New Brunswick, NJ 08901-1071
www.scils.rutgers.edu/ac/g/mls/
Master of Library Service

New Mexico
See Kansas, Emporia State University

New York
Long Island University
Palmer School of Library and Information Science
C. W. Post Campus
720 Northern Boulevard
Brookville, NY 11548-1300
E-mail: palmer@cwpost.liu.edu
www.liu.edu/palmer
Master of Science in Library and Information Science
Distance education opportunities: Manhattan; Westchester County

Pratt Institute
School of Information and Library Science
Information Science Center
200 Willoughby Avenue

Brooklyn, NY 11205
E-mail: info@sils.pratt.edu
www.sils.pratt.edu
Master of Science in Library and Information Science

Queens College
City University of New York
Graduate School of Library and Information Studies
65-30 Kissena Boulevard
Flushing, NY 11367
www.qc.edu/GSLIS/
Master of Library Science

St. John's University
Division of Library and Information Science
8000 Utopia Parkway
Jamaica, NY 11439
E-mail: libis@stjohns.edu
www.stjohns.edu/academics/sjc/depts/dlis/index.html
Master of Library Science

Syracuse University
School of Information Studies
4-206 Center for Science and Technology
Syracuse, NY 13244-4100
www.istweb.syr.edu
Master of Library Science
Distance education opportunities: Washington, D.C. (M.S.–Information Resources Management); Toronto (M.S.–Telecommunications and Network Management)
Short one-week residencies for core courses on Syracuse University Campus with Internet-based home study for course assignment completion.

University at Albany
State University of New York
School of Information Science and Policy
135 Western Avenue
Draper 113
Albany, NY 12222
E-mail: infosci@albany.edu
www.albany.edu/sisp/

Master of Library Science
Distance education opportunities: Poughkeepsie, New Paltz

University at Buffalo
State University of New York
Department of Library and Information Studies
534 Baldy Hall
Buffalo, NY 14260-1020
www.sils.buffalo.edu/dlis.htm
Master of Library Science
Distance education opportunities: Rochester (selected courses)
Internet (selected courses)
Two-way interactive video to Elmira (selected courses)

North Carolina

North Carolina Central University
School of Library and Information Sciences
1801 Fayetteville Street
P.O. Box 19586
Durham, NC 27707
www.slis.nccu.edu
Master of Library Science
Distance education opportunities: Fayetteville, Greenville, Hickory, Pembroke, Wilmington

University of North Carolina at Chapel Hill
School of Information and Library Science
CB #3360 100 Manning Hall
Chapel Hill, NC 27599-3360
E-mail: info@ils.unc.edu
www.ils.unc.edu
Master of Science in Library Science
Master of Science in Information Science

The University of North Carolina at Greensboro
Department of Library and Information Studies
School of Education
P.O. Box 26171
Greensboro, NC 27402-6171
www.uncg.edu/lis/
Master of Library and Information Studies
Distance education opportunities: Asheville, Charlotte

Ohio

Kent State University
School of Library and Information Science
Room 314 Library
P.O. Box 5190
Kent, OH 44242-0001
www.web.slis.kent.edu
Master of Library and Information Science
Distance education opportunities: Athens, Bowling Green (limited program on-site and via electronic distance learning), Cincinnati, Columbus (complete program on-site)

Oklahoma

University of Oklahoma
School of Library and Information Studies
401 West Brooks, Room 120
Norman, OK 73019-6032
E-mail: slisinfo@lists.ou.edu
www.ou.edu/cas/slis/
Master of Library and Information Studies
Distance education opportunities: Ardmore, Chickasha, Durant, Enid, Lawton, Tulsa, Weatherford

Oregon

See Kansas, Emporia State University

Pennsylvania

Clarion University of Pennsylvania
Department of Library Science
840 Wood Street
Clarion, PA 16214-1232
www.clarion.edu/libsci
Master of Science in Library Science
Distance education opportunities: Harrisburg, Southpointe
On-site or interactive television

Drexel University
College of Information Science and Technology
3141 Chestnut Street
Philadelphia, PA 19104-2875
E-mail: info@cis.drexel.edu

www.cis.drexel.edu
M.S. - Library and Information Science
Distance education opportunities: Internet

University of Pittsburgh
School of Information Sciences
505 IS Building
Pittsburgh, PA 15260
www2.sis.pitt.edu
Master of Library and Information Science

Puerto Rico

University of Puerto Rico
Graduate School of Information Sciences and Technologies
P.O. Box 21906
San Juan, PR 00931-1906
Master of Information Sciences

Rhode Island

University of Rhode Island
Graduate School of Library and Information Studies
Rodman Hall
Kingston, RI 02881
E-mail: gslis@etal.uri.edu
www.uri.edu/artsci/lsc
Master of Library and Information Studies
Distance education opportunities: Amherst, Boston, MA; Durham, NH
Internet, interactive video

South Carolina

University of South Carolina
College of Library and Information Science
Davis College
Columbia, SC 29208
www.libsci.sc.edu/
Master of Library and Information Science
Distance education opportunities: degree programs in selected states per contract arrangements

Tennessee

University of Tennessee
School of Information Sciences

804 Volunteer Boulevard
Knoxville, TN 37996-4330
www.sis.utk.edu
Master of Science
Distance education opportunities: admits students annually in the fall

Texas

Texas Woman's University
School of Library and Information Studies
P.O. Box 425438
Denton, TX 76204-5438
www.twu.edu/slis/
Master of Library Science
Master of Arts in Library Science
Distance education opportunities: Dallas
Interactive video: Corpus Christi, Edinburg, Texarkana, Tyler (a cooperative
with the University of North Texas)
Internet: selected courses

University of North Texas
School of Library and Information Sciences
P.O. Box 311068, NT Station
Denton, TX 76203-1068
www.unt.edu/slis/
Master of Science (2005)
Distance education opportunities: Minnesota; Houston, Lubbock, TX

The University of Texas at Austin
Graduate School of Library and Information Science
Austin, TX 78712-1276
E-mail: info@gslis.utexas.edu
www.gslis.utexas.edu
Master of Library and Information Science
Distance education opportunities: El Paso, San Antonio
Interactive television

Utah

See Kansas, Emporia State University

Virginia

See District of Columbia, The Catholic University of America

Washington
University of Washington
The Information School
Mary Gates Hall, Suite 370
Box 352840
Seattle, WA 98195-2840
E-mail: info@ischool.washington.edu
www.ischool.washington.edu
Master of Library and Information Science
Distance education opportunities: contact the Continuing Library Education
Specialist, UW Extension Office

Wisconsin
University of Wisconsin-Madison
School of Library and Information Studies
Helen C. White Hall
600 North Park Street, Room 4217
Madison, WI 53706
E-mail: uw-slis@slis.wisc.edu
www.polyglot.lss.wisc.edu/slis/
Master of Arts
Distance education opportunities: ETN, Web-based

University of Wisconsin-Milwaukee
School of Library and Information Science
Enderis Hall 1110
2400 East Hartford Avenue
Milwaukee, WI 53201
E-mail: info@slis.uwm.edu
www.slis.uwm.edu
Master of Library and Information Science
Distance education opportunities: Fox Valley, River Falls, WI; satellite sites
throughout the state of Wisconsin
Internet

Canada

Alberta
University of Alberta
School of Library and Information Studies
3-20 Rutherford South
Edmonton, AB T6G 2J4

E-mail: slis@ualberta.ca
Master of Library and Information Studies

British Columbia

The University of British Columbia
School of Library, Archival and Information Studies
1956 Main Mall, Room 831
Vancouver, BC V6T 1Z1
E-mail: slais.admissions@ubc.ca
www.slais.ubc.ca
Master of Library and Information Studies

Nova Scotia

Dalhousie University
School of Library and Information Studies
Faculty of Management
Halifax, NS B3H 3J5
E-mail: slis@is.dal.ca
www.mgmt.dal.ca/slis/
Master of Library and Information Studies (2005)

Ontario

University of Toronto
Faculty of Information Studies
140 St. George Street
Toronto, ON M5S 3G6
www.fis.utoronto.ca
Master of Information Studies
Distance education opportunities: Videoconferencing, Internet
See New York, Syracuse University

The University of Western Ontario
Graduate Programs in Library and Information Science
Faculty of Information and Media Studies
Middlesex College
London, ON N6A 5B7
E-mail: mlisinfo@julian.uwo.uwo.ca
Master of Library and Information Science

Quebec

McGill University
Graduate School of Library and Information Studies
3459 McTavish Street
Montreal, QB H3A 1Y1
E-mail: ad27@musica.mcgill.ca
www.gslis.mcgill.ca
Master of Library and Information Studies

Université de Montréal
Ecole de bibliothéconomie et des sciences de l'information
C.P. 6128, Succursale Centre-Ville
Montréal, Québec H3C 3J7
www.fas.umontreal.ca/EBSI/
Maîtrise en sciences de l'information

AMERICAN LIBRARY ASSOCIATION PERIODICALS

The focus of this book has been on career information for people who may be interested in librarianship or information science as a career. Their interest may be further stimulated and their quest for additional information satisfied by reading publications that are intended both for students and for those already in these careers. The many concerns and specializations within the library and information fields are not only reflected in, but often shaped by, the journals serving those areas. A review of any of these periodicals would provide anyone interested in these fields with ideas about current trends, major personalities, and general reports on the state of different parts of these career fields.

What follows is an alphabetical list of the various newsletters, magazines, and journals published within the American Library Association, including those available only over the Internet.

A brief profile is offered for each title, including the publishing frequency per year and availability of an on-line version. To order any of these periodicals, visit the ALA website at www.ala.org and click on "library" or contact: American Libraries, Subscription Department, American Library Association, S & S Computer Services, Inc., 434 West Downer Place, Aurora, IL 60506-9936.

ALA Washington News. ALA Washington Office. ISSN 1523-6005. Published at irregular intervals (minimum of twelve issues; more than twelve issues published if warranted by library-related legislation). Available on-line free of charge at www.ala.org/washoff/news.

ALCTS Newsletter Online. Association for Library Collections and Technical Services (ALCTS). ISSN 1523-018X. Published on-line only (four times a year); see www.ala.org/alcts/alcts_news/.

ALSC Newsletter. Association for Library Service to Children (ALSC). ISSN 0162-6612. Published quarterly. Sent to all ALSC members as part of membership. Not available by subscription.

American Libraries. The magazine of the American Library Association (ALA). ISSN 0002-9769. Published monthly except bimonthly June/July issue. Sent to all ALA members as part of membership. *American Libraries* is available to libraries and other institutions by paid subscription. No personal subscribers. On-line companion available at www.ala.org/alonline/.

Armed Forces Libraries Round Table of ALA Newsletter. Armed Forces Libraries Round Table (AFLRT). Published quarterly. Sent to all AFLRT members as part of membership. Not available by subscription.

base line. An official publication of the American Library Association's Map and Geography Round Table (MAGERT). ISSN 0272-8532. Published six times a year: February, April, June, August, October, and December. Sent to all MAGERT members as part of membership. Nonmembers may subscribe. Contact: *base line* Production Manager, Maps Library, Southwest Missouri State University, 901 South National, #175, Springfield, MO 65804-0095. Information available on-line at www.sunysb.edu/libmap/magert2. htm #baseline. Selections from the newsletter available in electronic form at *Electronic Publications: Digital base line.*

Book Links: Connecting Books, Libraries, and Classrooms. Magazine published by Booklist Publications, an imprint of the American Library Association (ALA). ISSN 1055-4742. Published bimonthly. Only available by subscription. Subscription inquiries should be sent to *Book Links*, Subscription Department, American Library Association, S & S Computer Services Inc., 434 West Downer Place, Aurora, IL 60506-9936. On-line companion available at the Book Links home page at www.ala.org/BookLinks/.

Booklist (Includes *Reference Books Bulletin*). Magazine published by Booklist Publications, an imprint of the American Library Association. ISSN 0006-7385. Published twice monthly September through June and monthly in July and August. Only available by subscription. On-line companion available at the Booklist Home Page at www.ala.org/ BookLinks/.

CHOICE. Association of College and Research Libraries (ACRL). ISSN 0009-4978. Published monthly except bimonthly in July/August; 11 issues. Only available by subscription. Contact the subscriptions department at subscriptions@ala-choice.org for information and special rates for subscribers outside North America. Subscription order form available. Subscription inquiries should be sent to Subscriptions, *CHOICE*, 100 Riverview Center, Middletown, CT 06457-3445, or call 860-347-6933. You may also fax 860-704-0465 for subscription services. On-line companion available at the CHOICE home page at www.ala.org/acrl/choice/home.html.

CLENExchange. Official publication of the Continuing Library Education Network and Exchange Round Table (CLENERT). Published quarterly. Sent to all CLENERT members as part of membership. Nonmember subscriptions available. Send subscription inquiries to ALA/CLENERT, 50 East Huron Street, Chicago, IL 60611-2795. Available on-line free of charge at www.ala.org/alaorg/ rtables/clene/clenexchange.html.

College & Research Libraries. Official journal of the Association of College and Research Libraries (ACRL). ISSN 0010-0870. Published bimonthly. Sent to all ACRL members as part of membership. Nonmember subscriptions available. Send subscription inquiries to *College & Research Libraries*, Subscription Department, c/o CHOICE, 100 Riverview Center, Middletown, CT 06457-3445. On-line companion available at www.ala.org/acrl/c&rl.html.

College & Research Libraries News. Association of College and Research Libraries (ACRL). ISSN 0099-0086. Published monthly except bimonthly July/August issue. Sent to all ACRL members as part of membership. Nonmember subscriptions available. Send subscription inquiries to *C&RL News*, c/o *CHOICE* subscriptions, 100 Riverview Center, Middletown, CT 06457-3445. On-line companion available at www.ala.org/acrl/c&rlnew2.html.

Counterpoise: For Social Responsibilities, Liberty and Dissent. Alternative review journal published by the Alternatives in Print Task Force of the Social Responsibilities Round Table. ISSN 1092-0714. Published quarterly. Only available by subscription. Send subscription inquiries to *Counterpoise*, 1716 SW Williston Road, Gainesville, FL 32608-4049. On-line companion available at www.liblib.com/Cpoise/Cpoise.html.

Documents to the People. Official publication of the Government Documents Round Table (GODORT). Published quarterly. Sent to all GODORT members on an annual basis as part of membership. Nonmember subscriptions available. For information contact Editor, Documents Librarian, University Library, 801 South Morgan Street, M/C 234, University of Illinois at Chicago, Chicago, IL 60607-7041. Information available on-line at DttP at http://govdoc.ucdavis.edu/~fzmeistr/dttp.html.

The EMIE Bulletin. Ethnic and Multicultural Information Exchange Round Table (EMIERT). ISSN 0737-9021. Published quarterly. Sent to all EMIERT members as part of membership. Nonmember subscriptions available. Send subscription inquiries to Publisher, EMIE Bulletin, Queens College, Graduate School of Library and Information Studies, 65-30 Kissena Boulevard, Flushing, New York 11367. On-line companion available at http://lonestar.utsa.edu/jbarnett/aboutbulletin.html.

The Federal Librarian. Federal Librarians Round Table (FLRT). Published four times a year. Sent to all EMIERT members as part of membership. Nonmember subscriptions available. Send subscription inquiries to 11 Battersea Lane, Ft. Washington, MD 20744. Information available on-line at FLRT "Federal Librarian" at www.ala.org/alaorg/rtables/flrt/fed lib.html.

Footnotes. New Members Round Table (NMRT). Published three times a year, in September, January, and April/June. Sent to all NMRT members as part of membership. Not available by subscription.

GLBTRT Newsletter. Gay, Lesbian, Bisexual, and Transgendered Round Table (GLBTRT). Published quarterly. Available by subscription to ALA members/institutions. Information available on-line at GLBTRT Clearinghouse and Newsletter Information at http://calvin.usc.edu/~trim mer/ala_clea.html.

IFRT Report.   Intellectual Freedom Round Table (IFRT). Published on irregular schedule. Sent to all IFRT members as part of membership. Not available by subscription.

Information Technology and Libraries.   Library & Information Technology Association (LITA). ISSN 0730-9295. Published quarterly. Sent to all LITA members as part of membership. Nonmember subscriptions available. Send subscription inquiries to *Information Technology and Libraries*, Subscription Department, American Library Association, S & S Computer Services Inc., 434 West Downer Place, Aurora, IL 60506-9936. On-line companion available at Information Technology and Libraries at www.lita.org/ital/index.htm.

Intellectual Freedom Action News.   Office for Intellectual Freedom (OIF). ISSN 0734-3086. Published monthly. Sent to members of the Chapter Intellectual Freedom Committees, the ALA Intellectual Freedom Committees, the Division Intellectual Freedom Committees, the Freedom to Read Foundation Board of Trustees, and Intellectual Freedom Action Network as part of membership. Nonmember subscriptions available. Send subscription inquiries to ALA OIF, 50 East Huron Street, Chicago, IL 60611-2795. Available on-line free of charge at Intellectual Freedom Action News at www.ala.org/alaorg/oif/ifan_pub.html.

Interface.   Official publication of the Association of Specialized and Cooperative Library Agencies (ASCLA). ISSN 0270-6717. Published quarterly. Sent to all ASCLA members as part of membership. Nonmember subscriptions available. Send subscription inquiries to *Interface*, Subscription Department, American Library Association, S & S Computer Services Inc., 434 West Downer Place, Aurora, IL 60506-9936. On-line companion available at the ASCLA Publications: Interface page at www.ala.org/ascla/ pubs.html.

International Leads.   Official publication of the International Relations Round Table (IRRT). ISSN 0892-4546. Published quarterly. Sent to all IRRT members as part of membership. Nonmember subscriptions available. Send subscription inquiries to International Relations Office, American Library Association, 50 East Huron Street, Chicago, IL 60611-2795. On-line companion available at International Relations Round

Table: Publications. Latest issue available on-line free of charge at www.ala.org/irrt/.

Journal of Youth Services in Libraries. Jointly supported official publication of the Association for Library Service to Children (ALSC) and the Young Adult Library Services Association (YALSA). ISSN 0894-2498. Published quarterly. Sent to all ALSC and YALSA members as part of membership. Subscription for nonmembers available. Subscription inquiries should be sent to *Journal of Youth Services in Libraries,* S & S Computer Services Inc., 434 West Downer Place, Aurora, IL 60506-9936. On-line companion available at JOYS on-line at www.ala.org/alsc/joys/index.html.

Knowledge Quest. An official journal of the American Association of School Librarians (AASL). ISSN 1094-9046. Published bimonthly September through May (five issues per year). Sent to all AASL members as part of membership. Subscriptions for nonmembers available. Subscription inquiries should be sent to *Knowledge Quest,* Subscription Department, American Library Association, 434 West Downer Place, Aurora, IL 60506-9936. On-line companion available at Knowledge Quest on the Web at www.ala.org/aasl/kqweb/index.html.

Library Administration & Management. Official journal of the Library Administration and Management Association (LAMA). ISSN 0888-4463. Published quarterly. Sent to all LAMA members as part of membership. Subscriptions for nonmembers available. Inquiries should be sent to Library Administration & Management, Subscription Department, American Library Association, 434 West Downer Place, Aurora, IL 60506-9936. On-line companion available at LA&M Magazine Home Page at www.ala.org/lama/la&m/index.html.

Library History Round Table Newsletter. Library History Round Table (LHRT). ISSN 0737-4984. Published semiannually. Sent to all LHRT members as part of membership. Not available by subscription. On-line companion available at Library History Round Table: Newsletters at www.spertus.edu/library-history/.

Library Instruction Round Table News. Library Instruction Round Table (LIRT). ISSN 0270-6792. Published quarterly. Sent to all LIRT members as part of membership. Not available by subscription. On-line companion available at Library Instruction Round Table News at http://web.uflib.ufl.edu/instruct/LIRT/lirt.html.

Library Resources & Technical Services. Official journal of the Association for Library Collections & Technical Services (ALCTS). ISSN 0024-2527. Published quarterly. Sent to all ALCTS members as part of membership. Subscriptions for nonmembers available. Subscription inquiries should be sent to *Library Resources & Technical Services,* Subscription Department, American Library Association, 434 West Downer Place, Aurora, IL 60506-9936. On-line companion available at LRTS online at www.ala.org/alcts/lrts/.

Library Systems Newsletter. Newsletter published by ALA TechSource, an imprint of the American Library Association (ALA). ISSN 0277-0288. Published monthly. Only available by subscription. Subscription inquiries should be directed to Circulation Manager, *Library Systems Newsletter,* ALA TechSource, 50 East Huron Street, Chicago, IL 60611-2795. Information, including a sample issue, is available on-line at www.ala.org/TechSourceALA/newsletter.html.

Library Technology Reports. Journal published by ALA TechSource, an imprint of the American Library Association (ALA). ISSN 0024-2586. Published bimonthly. Only available by subscription. Subscription inquiries should be mailed to Circulation Manager, Library Technology Reports, ALA TechSource, 50 East Huron Street, Chicago, IL 60611-2795. Information, including a cumulative index, is available on-line at www.ala.org/TechSourceALA/whatisit.html.

Meridian. Map and Geography Round Table (MAGERT). Published semiannually. Sent to all MAGERT members as part of membership. Nonmember subscriptions available. Write to Subscription Manager, *Meridian,* Map Collection, The University of Arizona Library, Tucson, AZ 85721. Information available on-line at www.sunysb.edu/libmap/magert2.htm#Meridian.

Newsletter on Intellectual Freedom. Office for Intellectual Freedom (OIF). ISSN 0028-9485. Published bimonthly (January, March, May, July, September, November). Only available by subscription. Subscription inquiries should be sent to *Newsletter on Intellectual Freedom,* Subscription Department, American Library Association, 50 East Huron Street,

Chicago, IL 60611-2795. Information available on-line at Newsletter on Intellectual Freedom at www.ala.org/alaorg/oif/nif_inf.html.

Prism. Office for Accreditation. ISSN 1066-7873. Published quarterly. www.ala.org/accreditation.html.

Public Libraries. Official journal of the Public Library Association (PLA). ISSN 0163-5506. Published bimonthly. Sent to all PLA members as part of membership. Nonmember subscriptions available. Subscription inquiries should be sent to *Public Libraries*, Subscription Department, American Library Association, S & S Computer Services Inc., 434 West Downer Place, Aurora, IL 60506-9936. On-line companion available at Public Libraries at www.pla.org/mag-index.html.

RBM: A Journal of Rare Books, Manuscripts, and Cultural Heritage. Association of College and Research Libraries (ACRL). Published twice a year. *RBM* is an independent ACRL publication. It is sent to members (and nonmembers) of ACRL's Rare Books and Manuscripts Section only with subscription order. Subscription inquiries should be sent to Subscriptions, CHOICE, 100 Riverview Center, Middletown, CT 06457-3445. Information available on-line at RBM at www.ala.org/acrl/rbmltxt.html and at Rare Books and Manuscripts Section at www.rbms.nd.edu/.

Reference Books Bulletin. Published in Booklist (see above) On-line companion available at Reference Books Bulletin at www.ala.org/booklist/v96/004.html.

Reference & User Services Quarterly. Official publication of the Reference and User Services Association (RUSA). ISSN 1094-9054. Sent to all RUSA members as part of membership. Subscriptions for nonmembers available. Subscription inquiries should be sent to *Reference & User Services Quarterly,* Subscription Department, American Library Association, 434 West Downer Place, Aurora, IL 60506-9936. On-line companion available at Reference & User Services Quarterly at www.ala.org/rusa/rusq/index.html.

RUSA Update. Official newsletter of the Reference and User Services Association (RUSA). ISSN 1095-2624. Published quarterly. Sent to all RUSA members as part of membership. Nonmember subscriptions available. Subscription inquiries should be sent to RUSA Update, S & S

Computer Services Inc., 434 West Downer Place, Aurora, IL 60506-9936. On-line companion available at RUSA Update at www.ala.org/rusa/update/.

School Library Media Research. An official journal of the American Association of School Librarians (AASL). ISSN 1523-4320. Published on-line only; see www.ala.org/aasl/SLMR.

SORT Bulletin. Staff Organizations Round Table (SORT). Published semiannually. Sent to all SORT members as part of membership. Not available by subscription.

SRRT Newsletter. Social Responsibilities Round Table (SRRT). ISSN 0749-1670. Published quarterly. Sent to all SRRT members as part of membership. Nonmember subscriptions available. Send subscription inquiries to *SRRT Newsletter,* American Library Association, 50 East Huron Street, Chicago, IL 60611-2795.

The Voice. Association for Library Trustees and Advocates (ALTA). Four issues a year. Sent to all ALTA members as part of membership. Not available by subscription. Issues on-line at The Voice at www.ala.org/alta/newsletter.html.

VRT Bulletin. Video Round Table (VRT). Published quarterly. Sent to all VRT members as part of membership. Not available by subscription. Some back issues available on-line free of charge at Video Round Table: Newsletter Archive at www.lib.virginia.edu/ dmmc/VRT/.

Women in Libraries. Feminist Task Force of the Social Responsibilities Round Table (SRRT). Published quarterly. Only available by subscription: $5 per year. Send subscription inquiries to Publisher, *Women in Libraries,* c/o American Library Association, 50 East Huron Street, Chicago, IL 60611-2795. Some selected articles available on-line at Women in Libraries at www.wtamu.edu/wil/.